EMERGENCY SURVIVAL

by
CHARLES A. LEHMAN

Illustrated by
DENNIS SMITH

"It's to the Point"

TECHNICAL BOOK CO.
2056 WESTWOOD BLVD.
LOS ANGELES, CALIF. 90025

PRICE $6.95 PLUS TAX
(Add $1.00 Postage/Handling)
PRIMER PUBLISHERS

i

ISBN 0-035810-03-X

FOREWORD

You were born with a strong will to live and you can maintain it in spite of fear, injury, cold, heat, starvation, dehydration, loneliness, or illness — especially if you have the knowledge and the tools to deal with them.

Emergency Survival is designed to give you the basics you need to survive an emergency in almost any environment. It's full of real-life examples, narratives, and illustrations. Many of the names and some of the locations have been disguised to avoid embarrassing the survivor or the unsuccessful survivor's survivors. There are some exceptions. Some cases have received so much publicity that trying to provide anonymity at this late date would be futile.

This text represents over twenty years of research and personal experience. Adventurer, author, educator, and survivor, Chuck Lehman has operated survival schools which have trained over 20,000 students. He is a pilot, diver, photographer, hunter, fisherman, backpacker, cross-country skier, snowmobiler, four-wheel drive buff, canoe enthusiast and log builder. The author has participated in both search and rescue operations and aircraft accident investigations. Late Vice President Humphrey once referred to him as the "survival expert". His work in survival education was recognized in 1977 by an award from the Survival and Flight Equipment (SAFE) Association.

CHAPTER	PAGE

**This survival book is endorsed by
The National Association of Search and Rescue**

1
SURVIVAL? WHO NEEDS IT?

IT WON'T HAPPEN TO ME

"Survival? Who needs it? Nothing's ever happened to me." "I'm no wilderness explorer or bush pilot. What do I care about survival?" These are some typical responses heard on the subject of this book.

Okay, no argument. You need the knowledge and skills outlined here *only* if you:

- Hunt
- Backpack
- Fish
- Ski
- Enjoy boating
- Birdwatch

- Travel by car
- Fly a light plane
- Live in an apartment
- Drive a dune buggy
- Drive a snowmobile
- Live in a suburb

People tend to think survival is a primitive "live off the

land" skill, needed by explorers, mountaineers, and fliers. Most assume that since they don't fit into one of those three categories, they do not need the skill.

Survival is really nothing more than managing your own mind and body in an unusual or hostile environment. Could you manage yourself in the following true-life situations?

- Dick and Jean drove to a hot spring near their home for a swim. An unseasonal snow began falling while they enjoyed the steaming water. By the time they returned to the parking lot, all the other cars were gone, and the road was slick. Their car slid off the pavement and got stuck. They made some mistakes — and Jean died. If they had known just a little about emergency survival, she might be alive.

- Picture yourself in your own home, surrounded by your family. A natural disaster (you pick the disaster most common in your area) isolates your house or apartment from its normal life support systems. Your electricity is off, the water system has been ruptured, and gas lines are broken. You have no heat, no air conditioning and no way to cook. All area roads are blocked. Rescue workers are tied up with people far worse off than you, and may not get into your neighborhood for several days. Every year hurricanes, earthquakes, tornadoes, blizzards or floods place town or city dwellers in real survival episodes. Those who know what to do make out just fine.

- A woman picking berries in Minnesota became disoriented in a wooded area. She spent two days and a frosty night looking for her car. During this time she followed some sound survival principles and was in fine shape when she walked up to her rescuers. She was over seventy years old!

- Four college students were returning to the campus after their Christmas break. They ran off an interstate highway in a blinding snowstorm. The next twelve hours were strictly an arctic survival situation even though they were less than fifty feet from the center line of a super highway. They made it — but only because the snowplow came along in the nick of time.

- A family of three was stranded in the mountains. They lost their lives in spite of a huge search effort — because they did not know how to signal the searchers.

  You could also find yourself in one of these situations. This time pick one of the alternatives suggested.

- It's a beautiful spring day, so you decide to leave work early and take a drive in the country. About eight miles from town, along a secluded road, you notice a picturesque tree-lined pond. There's no fence, and a footpath leads around the shore, so you decide to shed some years and be a kid again. Before long you're lost in memories, skipping pebbles off the glassy blue water. Then the rain starts. With little warning you are caught in a spring shower. In your dash to the car huge drops pelt you, soaking your permanent press clothes. By the time you reach for your keys the wind is blowing too. Through the water-beaded window you see a sickening sight — your keys dangling from the ignition switch. The doors are locked. You're shivering, mad at yourself — and in a typical survival situation. No mountains, no wilderness, no expedition, but what you do next may determine your future.

  You have probably seen the headlines, "John Doe Dies of Exposure." A lot of those incidents start as innocently as this spring drive. Would you . . .

3

a. Take shelter under a large, leafy tree near the road and wait for a passing motorist to help you.

b. Begin walking toward town. You can make the eight miles in about two hours of brisk walking, and will probably find help before going that far.

c. Break a car window with anything you can find and take shelter in your car.

d. Build a fire near the car and dry your clothes while you warm up.

The answer is c. Chapters 2 and 3 tell you why.

- Another example: Suppose you are driving from El Paso to Phoenix along Interstate 10. About noon the utter boredom of freeway driving and the haunting beauty of the desert tempt you to take a "short-cut." You take the first exit, drive south about five miles, then turn west on a well-maintained road. Paralleling the freeway is much more pleasant and your air conditioner keeps you in perfect comfort as mile after mile of colorful, blooming desert rolls by.

You check the rear view mirror to insure that this magnificent scenery is yours alone. No cars behind — but there is a white cloud billowing out behind the car. The bright red "HOT" light flashes on the instrument panel. Blown radiator hoses are common in the best of cars.

A blast of oppressing heat almost takes your breath away as you step from the driver's seat. One of the local radio stations mentioned a temperature of 115° just before you shut off the overheated engine.

But it feels much hotter. In the last hour you passed one ranch — about twenty-five minutes back, and met two cars — just after you left the freeway.

You are only about five miles from the freeway, but quite isolated. Another bona fide survival situation growing out of everyday life. How would you insure your survival in the searing desert heat . . .

    a. Begin walking toward the freeway and hail a passing car.

    b. Strip off as many clothes as possible to help beat the heat, then walk slowly back down the road looking for help.

    c. Stay in your car.

    d. Get in the shade, wait until dark, then walk out.

Again, the reasons are in chapter 2 and 3. This time the answer is d.

Survival situations can and do happen to average citizens, as well as to adventurous explorers. Everyone has the capability to handle them if they know and follow the principles in this primer.

If you believe "it _won't_ happen to me," perhaps the examples given show that it _could_ happen to you. Even if you are absolutely convinced your own good luck will keep you out of trouble, you will still find that knowing something about survival increases your enjoyment of all outdoor activities. If you like a drive through mountains or the desert, it is nice to know that no mechanical failure is going to get you into real trouble. If you prefer hiking in the woods, you'll find confidence in knowing a twisted ankle isn't going to cost you your life.

If you enjoy boating or canoeing, you will like it even more when you know that being driven ashore in some isolated spot by bad weather won't end up hurting one of your kids. If you fly your own plane, the knowledge that even a once-in-a-million mechanical failure need not mean unnecessary suffering, and that being forced down by weather can be comfortably endured.

People of all interests are flocking to schools dealing with survival-related subjects. Executives are sent to survival courses by their corporations, because the knowledge, confidence, and experience they gain help them deal with stress on the job.

This book is designed to get you started. The basics are here. Read it, project yourself into the scenarios, play the role, and you will find it's fun to learn about survival.

Finally, carry this primer in your backpack, car, boat, plane, or snowmobile as an extra confidence factor — a security blanket. If you should have a problem, it will coach and entertain you while you wait for rescue or for the weather to clear.

2
YOUR BODY IS
WHERE YOU LIVE

Survivors face many hazards, but only four present any immediate danger — heat, cold, dryness and injuries. If you enter your personal survival situation without getting hurt, or asphyxiated, there are three conditions which can pose immediate threats to your life (managing injuries is a separate subject, and is covered in chapter 11).

Hypothermia, hyperthermia, and dehydration are the three dangers. Prevent them and you are going to come home, little the worse for wear. All three boil down to taking care of your body — that is where you live.

Your body is something like the engine in your car. Supply it with the proper fuel, adequate cooling and efficient lubricants and it will run for years. Neglect any one of these, and you are headed for trouble.

Hypothermia is merely a lowering of the body's core

HYPOTHERMIA

THE LOWERING OF THE BODY'S CORE TEMPERATURE

WET

COLD

temperature. You are designed to operate at about 99° Fahrenheit. Drop that temperature even a few degrees and the machine starts to break down.

Suppose you have a flat tire on a lonely road at night. While you are struggling with the spare it starts to rain. There is a wind coming up, too. By the time you discover the spare is flat, you're soaked. It is very important that you make your destination before midnight, so you leave the car and walk two miles back down the road to a phone booth, to call a taxi.

By the time the dilapidated old cab finally pulls up, you are shaking like a leaf. You have never felt so cold. *That* is hypothermia — the newspapers call it "exposure."

You have probably experienced hypothermia at this level many times, so what's the big deal? Well, in a survival situation hypothermia is a killer — and a sneaky one at that.

Let's suppose there is no phone booth or that the taxi had not shown up. When you start to shiver, your body is sending a desperate signal. "Cover me up and feed me, I'm getting cold!"

Your body, like an engine, generates both energy and heat as it burns fuel. When you start to shiver, the body is telling you it is losing calories (heat) faster than they are being replaced. The shivering reflex exercises a whole bunch of muscles, and increases heat production, by burning more fuel. The fuel in this case is food.

Shivering alone is not likely to rewarm you. Active prevention is the key. If you have dry clothes, put them on. To produce heat, you can run in place, do calisthenics or isometrics to force your muscles to burn more fuel and generate heat.

In some survival situations when you opt to exercise, you are burning fuel you can't easily replace. You may not _have_ dry clothes to put on. Under survival conditions you have to _prevent_ hypothermia. Failing that, you must act fast. That means reducing heat loss as much as possible with a shelter, fire, and more clothing.

That seems fairly straight forward, doesn't it? But see what happens if you are slow to react or if you do not know what to do.

While you are shivering, the circulation to your hands and feet is being choked off. That is another automatic reflex to keep your vital organs warm. By reducing the flow of blood to your extremities, your body is reducing its loss of heat. But your hands and feet will get cold and stiff.

The last thing you need in a tight situation is clumsy hands. Those hands are going to have to build a fire, put up shelter, or button a coat. Ever try to strike a match with fingers stiff from cold?

As your core temperature continues to drop, you will stop shivering. That is a sure danger sign — and one you are not likely to recognize, because the biggest danger of hypothermia is that it takes away your will to help yourself. Amazing as it may seem, about the time you quit shivering you also quit worrying. You are dying and _you couldn't care less_.

At this point, your body loses the ability to rewarm itself. So, even if you have unlimited clothing or a thick sleeping bag to crawl into, you will continue to cool off. That means your only hope is adding heat. It could come from a warming fire, hot drinks – or another human body. One of the most effective ways of rewarming a hypothermia victim is in a sleeping bag with another person whose body temperature is still normal. Both bodies need to be stripped for adequate heat transfer to take place.

It is vital in a survival situation to prevent hypothermia, or at least to recognize it very early. You may not have a sleeping bag or a warm partner.

Prevent hypothermia by constantly thinking of your body as a heat producer with a limited supply of fuel. Use every means available to insulate yourself and stay dry!

If you have extra clothing with you, put it on before you start to shiver. Don't sit on or lean against rocks or metal vehicle parts. You will lose heat very rapidly through conduction. Get a fire going at the first hint of a chill. If possible, use more than one fire, so you can add heat from both sides. Drink all the hot fluids you can swallow. If you have extra food, use it to refuel and keep your body furnace going.

One final note on hypothermia — alcohol is _not_ a useful fuel. Your body will burn alcohol, but at the same time it will short circuit that automatic reflex which reduces blood flow to your extremities. As a result, just when your body is trying desperately to keep all that warm blood in close, near your vital organs, alcohol is opening the flood gates to your face, hands and feet. To make matters worse, alcohol slows your body processes — like generating heat. You will feel warm, but you will lose heat very fast, and your heart, lungs, and other internal organs will chill and quit. You may feel warm while you are dying. No alcohol!

At the other extreme of the quick acting dangers is hyperthermia. Overheating your body can be as disasterous as "over-temping" an engine — both can cause seizure of the machine. Fortunately, hyperthermia is not as common

HYPERTHERMIA

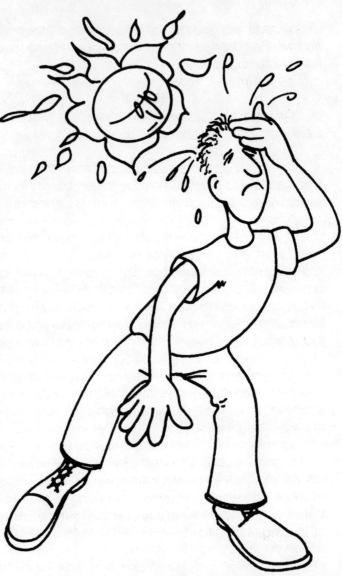

Overheating your body can be as disasterous as overheating an engine.

as hypothermia and is easier to prevent. Your body has a marvelous cooling system, capable of keeping your temperature stabilized around 99°F, even in the hottest desert. It can be overtaxed, though, unless you are careful.

While burning food heats your body, perspiration, breathing, and radiation cool it.

Let's say you were on an early morning hike in the desert between Barstow and Las Vegas, about ten miles off Interstate 15. You get disoriented. It is now noon and the temperature is 120°F. You are in no immediate danger — but wrong moves can do you in before morning.

Naturally, you are eager to get back to civilization and the lights and tables of Las Vegas. However, if you rush around trying to find your way, or set out for the highway, you can easily overtax your cooling system. If you work so hard that most of your sweat is running off rather than evaporating, your temperature will begin to rise. As it does, your body's heat-regulating mechanism in the brain ceases to function and shuts off your sweat. Your skin flushes and becomes dry. Suddenly, you collapse — the classic "heat stroke." Without treatment, death follows.

It is quite obvious that you cannot treat your own heat stroke. You have to prevent your temperature from getting too high. In hot weather that means severely limiting your physical activity, wearing your clothing loosely (but wearing it), staying in the shade, and drinking plenty of water.

The trouble is, survival conditions can impose serious limitations on your ability to do these things. You may have to build your own shade, you may not have "plenty of water." Still you should be aware of the danger of heat, and keep heat management high on your list of priorities.

Although heat stroke is the most dangerous form of hyperthermia, heat can also cause other problems, unless you act to prevent them.

Heat cramps can be painful and disabling. They are not true hyperthermia, because your body temperature may still be normal when they occur. If you have been working hard and sweating a lot, you are losing more than water. Even if your body can maintain its temperature, it will deplete its supply of water and salts (also called electrolytes, because when dissolved in water they form the conductive medium for electrical nerve impulses). You may drink plenty of water, but unless you also take in food or salt, the change in electrolyte balance may cause your muscles to cramp.

In a survival situation, you avoid cramps the same way you prevent true hyperthermia — by staying out of the sun and resting as much as possible. Sweat and salts are difficult to replace under survival conditions, so consider each a precious resource — too valuable to waste.

Perspiration is the common thread that ties together two of your immediate survival hazards: overheating and dehydration. Your body sweats to prevent hyperthermia, but even when it is successful, it dehydrates itself in the process. Unless you control this dehydrating effect, you can cause yourself an awful lot of grief.

Picture yourself after a successful forced landing in the northern U.S. in winter. Fortunately, you are dressed for the occasion, so hypothermia is no immediate threat. You scurry around all day building a snug shelter for you and your passenger. Both of you have worked hard on the lean-to and in gathering firewood for the night, but you were smart enough to avoid getting your clothes wet with sweat by stripping off a layer or two of clothes as you worked.

14

Around noon you each ate one of the sandwiches you had packed for the flight.

Your cheerful fire and cozy shelter have you feeling pretty good. "This survival business isn't bad at all. We're comfortable for tonight, and tomorrow there's sure to be someone out looking for us." Your partner does not answer, and seems unusually quiet. "Bill, what's the matter — you look sick." Bill doesn't look up, but mutters, "Yeah, it's my stomach. I feel like I'm going to lose that sandwich — and that's all the food we've got."

Sure enough, in the morning as you build a signal for passing planes, Bill starts vomiting and retching with dry heaves. By noon there is no rescue in sight, and you have a very sick partner.

If you were down in the Sahara Desert instead of the North Woods, you might suspect Bill's problem — and yours. It is water, or rather lack of it.

Dehydration is no respector of climates. Working vigorously in the cold, dry air, you and Bill were perspiring, but you did not notice, because your sweat evaporated quickly. Every breath you exhaled took some water vapor with it. In fact you saw those little vapor clouds as you breathed. Those beef sandwiches were delicious and good for you, but the handful of snow you washed them down with did nothing to help. Digesting the protein in the beef took far more water from your body than the snow added.

The cold made both of you urinate more often than usual, and each time your urine seemed darker than the time before. That was your one, easily seen sign that something was wrong.

You need a minimum of 3 quarts of water daily

DEHYDRATION

A LOSS OF 5% OR MORE OF YOUR BODY WATER IS DANGEROUS.

75% WATER

Dehydration is sneaky. There are early symptoms of the problem, but you are not apt to notice them if you are busy. A feeling of thirst is a very unreliable indicator. Oh, you'll get thirsty alright as you start to dehydrate. The problem is that just a few sips will often quench the thirst without improving your internal water deficit. Or you may not notice the thirst in the first place, because you are distracted. Being marooned in strange surroundings can be quite distracting.

If your natural thirst fails to spur you to drink enough water to rebalance your electrolytes, you will probably begin to notice a rather vague discomfort — again, not unusual for a survivor. As you use up more of your body's water, you will find it is more comfortable to move slowly or not at all than to hustle about your chores. If you glanced in a mirror you would notice your skin was a bit red, but you probably would pass that symptom off as sunburn, windburn or the glow that cold air puts on your cheeks. You will become impatient, too; but who wouldn't with no rescue in sight. So you still have no reliable indicator that all is not well.

Loss of appetite, increased pulse and respiration will also occur, but they are not likely to be noticeable, because your isolated situation will trigger the same responses.

At a water loss of about five percent of your body weight, you will get sick — just plain miserable. Waves of nausea will destroy all desire to drink. If you vomit, you will lose additional quantities of water. Then things start downhill in a hurry. You are losing fluid, you can't or won't drink, and the symptoms get worse.

As water loss continues, more noticeable symptoms will start appearing. You may get dizzy, have severe head-aches, shortness of breath, tingling extremities, a dry mouth, "thick" speech and be unable to walk. Dehydration at this level is extremely dangerous. You have to _prevent_ it.

In a survival situation water may be scarce or non-existent. If so, your safest bet is to be extremely stingy with the supply stored inside you. There is little you can do to reduce some water losses. You will lose almost two quarts of water each day through urination, breathing, and bowel movements. If you eat, more water will be used to digest the food. Eating is controllable so is the other big water thief — sweating. When you are a survivor, perspiration is your enemy. It robs you of the water supply stored in your body, and fouls up your electrolytic balance.

Unless you have lots of water available, eat sparingly and don't work up a sweat.

Protecting your body from hypothermia, hyperthermia and dehydration is your most critical challenge. You do it by managing your body as though it were a precious space-craft engine with very limited fuel, coolant and lubricant — the only engine that can get you home.

3
TAKE COVER

Shelter is a basic necessity of life. Without it, man and most of the higher animals are doomed. Many of the four-legged creatures of our woods and meadows must take their shelter as they find it or build one themselves. Our forebearers were proficient at both. Today, neither ability comes naturally. However, you are just as smart as your ancestors, and learning the skills of finding or building shelters is easy.

Let's go back to that spring drive in the country (from chapter 1). You are cold and wet, and you need shelter — fast. You could take cover under the trees, or build a lean-to, but since you are already wet, neither would provide what you want as quickly as you need it.

In this case your best shelter is your car. The only thing you have to improvise is a "key." Find a softball-sized rock or a sturdy section of log and smash the smallest, most vertical window which will allow you to reach a door lock or the keys. If the car is the hardtop style, you may be able to work a rattail comb, green twig, or stiff wire through the weather-stripping and lift the door lock. That will cause less damage, but it will also take time. Whenever you need shelter, one of the key points to remember is: Choose the shelter that will get you out of the weather most quickly.

Once you are inside the car, start the engine, turn on the heater to high heat and high fan. Plug up your entrance hole with whatever you have — floor mat, jacket, maps. As the car warms up, get those wet, synthetic fiber clothes off and wring them out — through a downwind window.

You are actually better off sitting in that warm car in the nude; but since you may not want to drive home that way, just replace the minimum number of items to make you presentable.

Okay, that was an easy one — but it illustrates some basic principles of shelters. Learn them, and all the rest will fall in line:

1. Recognize the need for shelter.
2. Take advantage of natural protection.
3. Try to locate the shelter so it will augment or replace the protection of your clothes.
4. Make provisions for heating or cooling.
5. Conserve your energy (don't build a log cabin when a lean-to will do).

All shelters have one basic purpose — to protect your body from overheating, overcooling or drying out. In other words, they prevent hyperthermia, hypothermia and dehydration.

We'll look at two types of shelters: natural shelters of opportunity and improvised shelters you build.

Most obvious in the natural class are vehicles. Probably more people get into "survival" situations while using vehicles than by all other means combined. Cars, boats, and airplanes all make very good shelters — under certain, limited circumstances. *If* they have fuel, are in running order, and have unobstructed exhaust systems, they can be excellent for general use. However, once the engine is dead they all have serious drawbacks. They are hard to heat and cool because they offer little insulation. On the other hand, they are relatively water and windproof.

So — to generalize. If wind or rain is your primary environmental threat, by all means use your vehicle. However, you *may* have to "modify" it a bit.

An example: Suppose you are driving across Nebraska on I-80 in December. It starts snowing and there is a strong northwest wind wafting the flakes across the highway. By mid-afternoon you are passing dozens of cars and trucks in the ditch. Other than a big semi-truck ahead, there is no traffic in sight. The wind is howling now, reducing visibility to a few yards, and a local radio station reports the temperature at +10°F with 60 MPH winds. Suddenly, a gust swings your car to the right, a wheel catches deeper snow and pulls you into the ditch. Snow is up to the door handles. For about fifteen minutes you sit there fuming and waiting for the highway patrol — or anyone. The wind temperature combination equates to a chill factor of about −40°F — arctic survival right on a main highway.

If you stay in the car, once you run out of gasoline the temperature inside will be virtually the same as outside — but without the wind. Because snow does a much better job of retaining heat than a car body does, a more effective shelter would be a snow cave. However, without arctic clothing and a shovel, the wind is going to hurt you before you can dig a full-fledged snow cave. Without arctic clothing you have two options — stay in the car or build a modified snow cave.

If you elect to stay in the car, here are some guidelines:

— Run the engine for about ten minutes every hour. *Caution:* carbon monoxide is a danger here. Make sure the tail pipe is clear and that the wind is blowing the exhaust fumes away from the car.

— Set the heater control to circulate fresh air from outside and place the heater blower on high. By running the heater blower on high and pulling in outside air, you will pressurize the inside of the vehicle slightly. This helps keep engine exhaust out. However, be sure the exhaust is not blowing across the heater air intake (usually just in front of the windshield).

— If your car uses a recirculating style heater (check the owner's manual), keep a downwind window slightly open when the engine is running.

Your second option is really a further refinement of the first. If you have enough gas to run your car heater for awhile, good warm clothes, and a digging tool, you can combine the best features of the windbreak provided by the car and the insulation of the snow cave.

Leave the shelter of your car *only* for short periods to work on a snow cave, and return to warm up as soon as you get cold or notice any numbness of face, hands, or feet.

SNOW
CAVE

Under high wind conditions your work periods will be very short, so do not attempt an "outside" shelter unless you have plenty of gas for those warm-up breaks.

Regardless of whether you stay in the vehicle or move to a snow cave, you are going to need all the insulation you can get. The most obvious source is clothing. If you have suitcases in the trunk, get them out *as soon as you are stuck*. The drifts will soon deny you access to the trunk. People have died of hypothermia in their cars with a trunk full of warm clothes.

Another good source of insulation is the interior of the car. However, to take advantage of it you have to get it closer to you. That may mean pulling up the floor mats to wrap your feet or carpet the snow cave, or removing the roof lining (head-liner) for a blanket. By all means take the rear seat if you move to a snow cave. It is far better insulation than a snow bench and will keep you warmer.

The stuffing in your seat cushions is an excellent insulator. By cutting open the seats and using the roof lining, you can make an effective sleeping bag. If all this damage sounds expensive — it is. But, the alterative is much worse. The folks who make the headlines after every blizzard might have been anonymous, and alive, if they would have just used what they had.

One final word on cars as arctic-type shelters. In a blizzard, DO NOT TRY TO WALK OUT! Stay in or next to your car even if you passed a farm house only a mile back. The cold, the wind, deep snow and poor visibility will combine to disorient you, exhaust you, and kill you. Walk out *only* if a safe haven is *in sight*, is never obscured by blowing snow, and is close enough so you *know* you can make it. Then walk only if you have really warm clothes.

The same ideas apply to light aircraft except it is unlikely you will have use of the engine and heater if you have been forced down. You can strip a lot of insulation and shelter from the cockpit, or you can stay inside if wind is your most dangerous problem. Lauren Elder was the sole survivor of an above-timberline crash in the Sierra Nevada because she used the shelter of the aircraft warmed with rocks heated in a fire.

Cars, boats, and planes make fine shelters from the wind and rain. In the desert scenario, from Chapter 1, the car is a good shelter; since your first need on the desert in the summer during daylight is shade. Without shelter the sun will overheat and dehydrate you.

Unfortunately, the shade you get inside your car is of little help — it's like a shady oven. Use the shade outside your car. Depending on the sun angle, that may mean crawling under the car — no easy task on some low-slung models. There is usually some place to squeeze under, though. Use a hub cap to dig away a few inches of dirt. Watch out for hot exhaust pipes. Airplanes too, are better ovens than shade trees; but it is usually easy to use wing or tail surfaces for protection from the sun.

On the shores of our Southwestern desert lakes the combination of shade from a disabled boat and cooling from the lake water (splashed onto your clothes) almost eliminates the hazard of desert heat. Again, the only safe survival decision is to stay with the boat and use its shelter and equipment.

Vehicles are effective shelters within their limitations. However, other, made-to-order shelters provide better protection.

Most romantic, of course, are wilderness cabins. Who hasn't read of some hapless wanderer stumbling through the snow finding a fully stocked log cabin. Such cabins do exist — in some parts of the country. Finding one is highly unlikely. On the other hand, man-made "shelters" dot the sides of nearly every road. Barns, corncribs, cattle shelters, hay or straw stacks, abandoned houses, or even houses whose owners are away have all saved cold, tired, wet or overheated travelers. All of these fit the five basic principles of shelters.

In 1976, I took part in the search for a retarded, fifteen year old boy who had wandered away from an outing. The weather was terrible — cold rain, intermittent snow, wind, and standing water were everywhere. Conditions were per fect for hypothermia, and this lad had the mental age of a two year old, so we expected the worst. All night about one hundred searchers combed half a dozen square miles of forest, lake shore, and wheat fields without success. By dawn, hope was fading for the lightly clad boy. Then he was found, asleep, dry and warm. When the rain started, he'd crawled into the hay inside an old barn. His natural inclination to curl up and go to sleep when he got cold had saved him.

Most people would have been embarrassed at being lost so close to home and probably would have tried to walk out, getting soaked and hypothermic in the process. Sometimes, man-made structures can provide all the protection you need in any weather if you will just admit you need shelter and use all your ingenuity to find and use it.

Consider that Nebraska blizzard used as an example earlier in this chapter. If your car had stalled within sight of one of the many straw or haystacks along I-80, you would be able to wait out the storm in far more comfort than in your car or a snow cave. Imagine the snug shelter you could build from hay bales in just minutes.

You might have to collapse part of the stack to get "building blocks," but you could have a dry floor, thick walls with a foot or more of insulating, dry, dead air space, and a watertight, insulated roof.

Culverts and bridges can provide shelter along roads or railroads. Naturally, some of them are so located as to be subject to flash flooding. If you must seek shelter under a bridge or in a culvert, stay alert and have an escape route planned if water should begin rising dangerously.

Caves and rock overhangs make excellent shelters from heat, cold, wind, or water. They provide cool shade in the desert and, when equipped with a proper fire, they can be almost permanent shelters — which apparently they were for a considerable part of man's history. One of the best night's sleep I ever had was on the sandy floor of a 10 by 40 foot rock cave. It faced west, and the afternoon sun had warmed the sand and rock, which stayed warm all night and kept me comfortable.

In spite of their comfort and natural attraction, caves demand a bit of caution. Watch out for "caves" or holes in clay or gravel banks. They have a habit of collapsing during wet weather. The same goes for caves or overhangs with loose rocks over head. If you are in a predicament that calls for using a cave as shelter, you are _not_ on a cave exploration jaunt. Don't go beyond sight of the entrance!

Hollow trees and logs were used by our ancestors as shelters and even temporary homes. While logs big enough for permanent dwellings are very rare now, a casual search of almost any woods will usually turn up a tree or log with enough of a cavity to allow you to squeeze in. They can provide a dry place to rest, at least some insulation, and a ready supply of firewood which can often be stripped away from the inside with a knife.

Again, a word of caution. It is nice to have company in a survival situation — but before you plunge into some cosy wooden cavity, check it out. Sometimes the "critters" that live there would not make good roommates. You may be able to evict them but be careful who you try to displace, and how you go about it.

An entire book this size could be devoted to improvised shelters, because there are an almost unlimited number of styles and modifications. So we'll limit this discussion to a few easy-to-build styles which can be modified to suit the weather, terrain or personal whims.

One of the easiest and most versatile of all shelters is the simple lean-to. It can be built of almost any material, in a variety of situations. A well built lean-to will provide a dry, roomy shelter that can be heated with a fire. You *can* build a lean-to with no tools or man-made materials, but it is easier if you always carry a few yards of cord and a knife.

A lean-to is nothing more than a steeply-sloping roof (about 60°) that extends all the way to the ground. It may have sides if you wish. You can build one from poles, cover it with boughs, bark, blankets, floor mats, grass, the hood from your car, poncho, rain coat — even an animal skin. Lacking poles, you can support your lean-to from the side of your car, a tree, rocks, ski poles, etc.

Lean-tos are fast, easy and adaptable. The roof should be steep enough to shed rain, high enough to let you sit comfortably, and wide enough so you can stretch out parallel to the entrance if you are alone or from front-to-back if you have company. Place the rear of the lean-to against the wind, so you can put a fire in front without worrying about smoke. If there is a significant wind, close in the rear.

You can get as fancy as you like with a lean-to, but remember, the reason you are building the shelter is to conserve and preserve the energy you are carrying within you — so don't _waste_ energy building a fancy shelter. A crude but protective shelter covering a rested and healthy body is far better than a textbook-perfect shelter containing an exhausted survivor.

Nowhere does the KISS principle apply better than in survival — "Keep It Simple, Survivor."

With that in mind, let's look at some even more rustic shelters.

If you have ever walked through a woods, you've seen the basic structure for several easy shelters. When big trees are blown over, they often lift a large, relatively flat "pan" of roots out of the ground. Unless the ground is very wet, you can use the pit that the roots were pulled out of as the floor of a fine shelter. However, during prolonged heavy rain the pit will collect water. On the other hand, it can be a super shelter in cold winter weather. The pit will probably be full of leaves or needles — good floor insulation. Use the up-ended root pan as one wall of your shelter and lean logs, sections of bark, or branches against the wall.

To make your shelter waterproof, you can "shingle" it with overlapping boughs or bark slabs, beginning at the bottom and working upwards. Keep the door small and try to make your shelter as watertight and well insulated as available materials and your energy will permit.

If there is snow on the ground, this is a fine shelter to "thermalize." You can make it snug as an igloo by piling at least eight inches of loose snow over the primary structure. Then plug the doorway with spare clothing, a block or ball of snow, or a pack or bag of loose snow. This is important when you cannot get a fire going for heat.

The snow cave is highly effective when there is enough of the right kind of snow. You can make them quite exotic with raised sleeping platforms and cold air sumps, all carved out of snow. However, any cave you can dig into snow without getting yourself wet or exhausted will serve you well. The important thing is not to waste time and energy getting fancy. A snow cave kept three boys alive and well on Oregon's Mount Hood for over two weeks in a raging blizzard.

For really cold weather there is a refinement to the principle of snow insulation. You can make any of the snow-covered shelters warmer by using the natural heat that radiates from the earth. Even in arctic perma-frost areas, the frozen earth actually radiates some heat. By scraping away all snow and ice from the frozen ground inside your shelter, you can take advantage of it.

Near Fairbanks, Alaska, in 1973 I observed a thermalized double lean-to just big enough for one person. The ground inside it was bare and the shelter had been empty overnight — so no body heat could have affected the demonstration. Yet at 9:00 in the morning the outside temperature was 31° below zero — while inside the empty shelter a thermometer read 0°F. That's a big difference! A second, identical shelter was occupied throughout the night. Its inside temperature was a comfortable 26°F.

Another, almost-natural shelter can be made from the trunk of a fallen tree. Use a tree that rests high enough off the

FALLEN TREE SHELTER
hollow out and
thatch outside

deep snow

TREE WELL SHELTER

ground to allow you to sit under or beside it. First make _sure_ the tree won't roll over. Use the log as a ridge pole, and build a double lean-to out of small logs, bark, boughs, blankets, etc.

When heavy snow falls in coniferous forests, there is usually little drifting, so the snow stays light, powdery and uniformly deep — to the joy of skiers, snowmobilers, and snowshoe enthusiasts. This phenomenon literally builds shelters at the base of thick evergreens with low branches. Snow sticks to or slides off the branches leaving a "well" in the deep snow at the base of the tree trunk. Tree wells may be several feet deep, with steep, inverted bell-shaped sides. If you need fast winter shelter, they are hard to beat. You may want to hallow out a spot for your feet and improvise some sort of roof, but at least the "tree well" provides immediate protection; you can make refinements later.

A few years ago two young skiers got lost on Mount Spokane in Washington. They had no survival gear, wore only fairly light ski togs and had very little training. Temperatures were far below freezing. Yet when the boys were found nearly twenty-four hours later, they were in fine shape — in fact they were better off than some of the searchers. The reason — the twelve year olds took shelter in a tree well; while the searchers combed the mountain, exposed to wind and cold. It was quite natural for the kids to make a "snow house," but a pair of hunters lost on another mountain didn't follow that natural inclination. Both became statistics.

All this woodsy stuff is fine, if you are "lucky" enough to meet your survival situation in the great outdoors, but what if your problem occurs at home? Your house or apartment is a fair shelter — from some things. But if you lose all utilities in the dead of winter, the insulation will only serve to keep day-time and nighttime temperatures more uniform. That is, your house will probably be colder than outside during the day and a bit warmer than outside at night. Not a very comforting thought. Even with a whole family inside, body heat is going to have little effect. Your shelter is simply too big.

So the secret to comfort inside an unheated house is much the same as in the piney woods — make your shelter only as large as necessary. There are many ways to make your house "smaller".

First, select one room as your shelter. Naturally, one with a fireplace is ideal, but not necessary. A room with south facing windows will allow you to capture some solar heat during the day (pull the drapes at night). Close off your shelter room from the rest of the house.

If you still cannot heat the whole room, make your shelter still smaller — like your ancestors did. When the cabin got too cold, they stayed in bed. A bed is a fine shelter, especially if there are two or more people in it, and you pile on the covers. You can also build a smaller room within the shelter room. Tents. cabanas, lean-tos all work well inside a house or apartment. Construction materials are all around you. Blankets, rugs, sofa pillows, sheets, plastic tarps, rope, electrical cords, clothes pins — ad infinitum.

A small booth or tent, built against a wall containing a fireplace is one of the most comfortable cold weather shelters imaginable. Four of us spent two cozy, happy days lazing in front of a crackling fire in an unheated house during a howling, sub-zero Duluth blizzard a few years back. We were sorry when the power came back on and the plows came through!

Your home can serve as a shelter from natural disasters, too. Just be prepared to adapt it to your needs. There are no "pat" rules for survival shelters — only principles that must be adapted to _your_ situation.

4
FIRE UP

Searchers found the lost hiker in less than twenty-four hours. He was sitting against a large tree surrounded by the butts of about two packs of cigarettes and dozens of burned matches. He'd been dead for only a few hours.

This robust, healthy American lost his life under relatively mild weather conditions and while he had everything necessary to survive comfortably. Why?

He simply gave up, quit, stopped working at the business of living. The thought of being lost in the wilderness overwhelmed him, so he sat down and died.

Incredible? Yes, but it happens far too often.

Volumes have been written about the "will to live," "positive mental attitude," and its importance in survival. One simple act does more for a survivor's peace of mind than any other — building a cheery fire.

Fire is useful to warm the body, but has other benefits too. Dancing flames warm the heart, cheer the soul, and lift the mind. That's a big return from a simple oxidation process.

If the lost hiker had used one of his matches to start a fire, he would have found the fearful world around him far less menacing. It is hard to stay scared or depressed while you watch flames dance.

Ask any boy or girl scout, "What are the elements necessary for a fire?" They will probably say, "Heat, fuel, and oxygen." That is simple enough. Anyone should be able to combine those elements and start a fire. You can too — *if* you really understand the chemical reaction involved.

For example: If you want to start a fire with a match and some half-inch twigs, what is your fuel? Careful! This is a trick question. The twigs are not really fuel. Fires burn gases, not solids or liquids. The things we *call* fuels burn only when they are heated enough to vaporize the combustible elements.

When you completely grasp that concept, fire building becomes easier. One match cannot heat half-inch sticks enough to vaporize them.

Let's take an easy-to-build fire and see how it works. Suppose you are hiking on a mountain trail and want a fire to brew some afternoon tea. You are below timberline so there is plenty of wood. Your lunch is wrapped in waxed paper and you have a reliable cigarette lighter in your pocket.

Step into the woods and gather an armful of dead

branches (squaw wood) from the lower trunks of standing trees. Select a dry, level spot, out of the wind and _build_ your fire. You build the fire first — then you light it.

Crush the waxed paper into loose balls, and lay them on a flat rock, or dry ground. Break some of the smallest twigs (1/8 inch or less) and stand them teepee fashion against the paper balls. Add some larger twigs (1/4 inch) taking care to leave space between them. These natural chimneys should be almost as wide as the sticks. Continue with your teepee until you have one-inch sticks all the way around, separated by appropriate chimney spaces.

Now, hold a flame under the paper balls. Since the tip of the flame is hottest, hold the lighter so the flame tip touches an exposed edge of the waxed paper. Within a minute you will have a blazing, relatively smokeless fire.

Okay, that was too easy, but it demonstrates the principles. To produce fuel gases by vaporizing wood, you need either a big heat source or small wood. That is always true. If you want a survival fire, you will need a reliable source of intense heat, some very fine fuel material called tinder, and some sustaining "fuel." For ease of discussion, we will call the solid matter "fuel" — but remember, gases are the _real_ fuel.

Arrange the tinder, kindling and fuel so each heats the other and adjacent pieces heat each other.

The best survival heat source is the one you carry with you. Forget about exotic stuff like rubbing sticks together, striking sparks from hard rocks, or concentrating the sun's heat with eye glasses or camera lenses. All of these methods will start a fire — but _not_ under typical emergency conditions which would cause you to _need_ a fire.

Tinder is the second ingredient in the fire chain. You will need it for every fire. It is often easiest to carry your own. Tinder must be easy to heat enough to release fuel gases. Good tinder has lots of exposed surface area and a very thin cross section. You can use any substance that will magnify and sustain your original heat source until the larger fuel begins to vaporize.

In our example, the waxed paper was an effective tinder, but we could have used dry moss from the same tree that supplied the squaw wood. Or we might have used shredded cedar bark, cattail fuzz, birch bark or even a dollar bill.

One common tinder is worthy of special mention because it is so widespread and so effective. "Indian Kerosene," more commonly known as pitch, is available anywhere that evergreens grow, from Florida pines to the Alaska forests. All conifers "bleed" when they are injured. The pitch hardens upon contact with air and forms globs of golden brown, glassy-looking fire starter. It is easy to find and easy to use.

If you scrape a lump of pitch with your knife, nail clipper, file, or car keys, the resulting shavings will ignite easily and burn for a long time. Lay a lighted match on quarter-sized piles of pitch and it will burn for several minutes. Or you can just break off a chunk of pitch, lay it at the base of your fire and ignite one edge with your lighter. The lump will begin to melt and burn even hotter until it is consumed. The nicest thing about pitch is that it works well wet or dry.

Another "weather proof" natural tinder is birch bark. It is fairly widespread and as easy to use as dry paper — even after days of rain.

TINDER

KINDLING

FUEL

41

Pitch wood is also excellent. You will find it in the sharp spires that stick up from the stumps of coniferous trees felled by wind or saw. Kick one of these thin spines over; cut into it and you will notice yellow-brown wood that is unusually heavy and smells of turpentine. You can shave it and use it like pitch or sliver it and use the thin strips "cross-hatched" or teepee fashion. Either way, it burns great.

With a heat source and some tinder in hand, it is time to look for some kindling. In order to vaporize heavier fuel, you will need some transition fuel to further magnify the heat of your tinder. Kindling can be twigs of pencil size, or slivers split from larger pieces of wood. It should be as dry as possible and graduated in size up to about one-inch in diameter.

Fuels for survival fires run the gamut from the obvious to the bizarre. We all tend to think about neat dry logs crackling into clean, orange flames — but even your spare tire may provide the smoking, stinking heat that saves your life. So it is best to let your imagination free-wheel a bit.

If you have the choice, nice dry hardwood makes the best fire. However, survivors usually can't be choosers, so use what you have. Just get plenty. Always gather more fuel than you think you could possibly need. You will be amazed at the prodigious appetite of even a small fire — and chances are in a survival situation you won't have a small fire. The tendency is to build a big, comforting blaze, but . . .

Survival instructors quote an anonymous native American who made fun of "White Man's Fires." "The Indian makes a small fire, sits close, stays warm. White man builds big fire, sits back — and stays warm carrying more wood." Whoever he was, he was right. In a survival situation staying warm by carrying wood burns vital energy that you may not be able to replace. Let the fire work for you.

Make every attempt to gather your wood from above the ground. Dead branches from standing trees or dead logs suspended above the forest floor will almost always be drier than wood gathered from the ground.

If wood is scarce in the spot your emergency chooses to happen, don't despair; there are other fuels and tinders. In desert-like areas dry sage and other brush burns very well. You can usually find enough for a small fire to get you through a cold night. Dry grass can be highly effective as both tinder and fuel for a survival fire. Even in soggy tundra I have cooked over a fire of grass bundles. Sea and lake shores often abound with driftwood, which is excellent fuel.

If you are marooned with your vehicle, you can burn gasoline, motor oil, tires and floor mats. Gasoline is not ideal fuel for open fires. In fact, it is downright dangerous; but if you really *need* a fire, gasoline is less dangerous than hypothermia. You should use caution, though.

If you have tools, you can disconnect a fuel line or drain the crankcase and collect the gasoline and oil in hub caps, rags, bottles, etc. Without tools it is more difficult, but you can still get at the gasoline. Use a knife or the jack handle to puncture the fuel tank. That may take some doing, but it is possible. Catch the gasoline and move it at least 25 feet crosswind from the car. If possible soak some sand, dry dirt or rags with the gasoline, then ignite it from the upwind side, using your free arm to shield your eyes and face. Expect a large flash before you get the match or lighter all the way to the gasoline. No external heat is required to vaporize gasoline, so the "fuel" is really floating around in the air *near* the liquid.

Never add more gasoline to a survival fire. If the fuel is running low in one fire, carry gasoline to a new spot several feet away crosswind, then carefully carry a burning bit of dirt or stick to the new gasoline supply, using the same precautions. Pouring gasoline into a fire is a sure way to get hurt!

CAUTION: Do not fool around with gasoline fires in practice sessions. They're too dangerous. However, when you _need_ a fire and have nothing else, just remember — fuel is wafting around in the air, ready to burn explosively, so watch the wind.

Oil fires are built the same way, with saturated sand, etc. Or you can use motor oil as an assist for igniting wet wood. Motor oil is safe to work with and very effective.

Animal droppings make a useful fuel. Dry cattle or horse dung burns fairly well, and is often found far from any other fuel. Frontiersmen learned to use "buffalo chips" to cook their coffee when nothing else was available.

Since we _build_ fires, it seems logical that architecture should be important, and it is. By selecting the right architectural style you can insure a fast-starting, hot-burning fire every time. Get careless and that magic mix of heat, fuel and oxygen will go awry. The trick is to arrange the material so that each burning piece heats and supports the one next to it but lets air flow between.

The teepee is the basic style to start nearly all wood fires. It can be used for any sized fire, but has a tendency to collapse randomly and require rearranging.

The log cabin fire is easy to build, more stable, and

TEEPEE FAST FIRE

LOG CABIN

SLOW BUT SURE

GRID
LOTS OF COALS

45

requires less tending. To make it, just lay a log on each side of a tinder-and-kindling teepee. Set two more logs across the ends of the first two and continue to add levels, log cabin fashion. It is best to lean the walls inward a bit and lay a flat, log roof on top, being sure to leave air spaces between the roof logs. The nice thing about a log cabin fire is that the natural chimney that insures good burning is automatic.

Another modification that works very well is the grid or cross-grate fire. Support a row of kindling sticks parallel to each other and just above your tinder, leaving spaces between them equal to their diameter. Place the next layer at right angles, using the same concept. Continue, making each layer of larger material. This style has one big advantage. It concentrates the fuel near its center providing a large bed of hot coals, as opposed to the log cabin's rather hollow blaze with few coals in the center. It's easy to convert a log cabin to a grid a few layers up. This gives you the log cabin hollow for your tinder and the grid's concentrated coals.

If you want a fire that will heat a lean-to or keep you warm while you sleep, build a long fire. Drag two long, preferably green logs to your campsite and lay them parallel about 18 inches apart in front of your shelter.

Use a teepee, log cabin, or grid structure to start a fire between the logs; then spread the fire gradually until you have a fire six feet long. In addition to providing heat over the length of your shelter, this type of fire makes it easy to burn long logs. That means you don't waste energy cutting or breaking wood. Just shove the logs into the fire from each end and feed them further in as they burn.

Another way to avoid breaking wood is to convert the teepee or log cabin to a star fire; push long logs into the fire from all sides until they meet in the middle. Then feed them into the fire as they burn.

Any fire can be improved by placing a reflector behind it. Rocks or green logs can be stacked to prevent total escape of heat from the back of your fire. They won't reflect a lot, but they help. One caution: Do not use water-soaked, porous rocks in or near the fire. As they heat up, trapped steam may explode them. Probably the best reflector is an aluminized mylar blanket. They are sold under various trade names. Sparks from the fire will burn holes and they will melt if you get them too close to the flames, but stretching one vertically a couple of feet behind the fire will cause a noticeable increase in the heat radiated into your shelter.

Fire building is easy when conditions are ideal. When they are not, you must apply all the principles properly to get one going. ALWAYS, always carry a fire starter when you are in the outdoors. The most versatile fire starters are lighters and matches. There are many commercial kits available, but those that provide both easy lighting and hot burning tinder are best.

Be sure the lighter or matches you carry will work when you need them. That means the lighter has to be reliable, preferably the butane type with a visible fuel supply. If you prefer matches, carry the strike-anywhere type in a water-proof container that you can open — even with cold, wet hands. One of the most popular ones on the market is excellent for keeping matches dry, but virtually impossible to open with cold hands. The new waterproof-windproof wooden matches with the extra long heads are a worthwhile investment.

You can make tinder by filling a 35mm film can with

cotton balls and soaking them with lighter fluid, then screwing the top on tightly and sealing with plastic tape. The saturated cotton will stay soaked for about a year when properly sealed and will burn for several minutes when placed at the base of a stack of other tinder and ignited. Candle stubs, jellied-petroleum products, wax-impregnated wood strips, fuel pellets, and fuel-soaked fiber are all excellent tinder. If you prefer going primitive, just carry a chunk of pitchwood or a piece of pitch in a little plastic bag.

One final note on fires: If you get into trouble and need heat or light — or comfort — build a fire *immediately*. Don't wait. The colder, wetter or more scared you get, the tougher it is. Stack the odds in your favor. Make your first effort good; do it right — no shortcuts. Gather and arrange your tinder, kindling, and fuel, then fire up.

A lost hunter spent several days in the Alaskan wilds. When his rescuers walked into his makeshift camp, he was standing next to his fire turning a rack of roasting caribou ribs. He greeted them with, "Hey, you guys had lunch, yet?" What's better than that?

TINDERS

NATURAL	MAN MADE
* Birch bark	* Candle stubs
Cedar bark	* Insect repellent
Dry tree moss	Cotton cloth
Pitchwood shavings	Gasoline or oil soaked sand
* Resin shavings	Waxed paper
* Pitch shavings	Oily rags
Dry pine needles	* Birthday candles
Dry leaves	Paraffin soaked wood strips
Rotted wood	Paper money
Bird nests	Cigarette or pipe lighters
Cattail fuzz	Smokeless powder
Termite nests	* Magnesium shavings
Dead bamboo	Cotton balls
Dry grass	Lint

Note: Tinders marked with an asterisk are usable wet or dry.

5
MAKE A FUSS

Alvin and Phyllis Oien and their daughter Carla Corbus found themselves marooned in snow-covered, mountainous terrain. The forced landing of their light plane had injured the Oiens, but not critically. Search planes flew almost six hundred hours over the area. Phyllis and Carla kept a diary while huddled in their plane — just eight miles from a U.S. highway — for at least fifty-four days. Alvin had left after a few days to go for help. They were all extremely brave and courageous — but they all died. There was no evidence that they ever tried to signal the search planes which repeatedly flew overhead.

If you are in trouble and need help, you have to *ask* for it. You must tell the world. Even if you are a master of survival skills and capable of living off the land indefinitely, you still need to signal your fate and location to the outside world.

Signaling is not difficult. However, it does require some

preparation or some on-the-spot ingenuity. Basically, all signals fall into three categories; visual, aural, and electronic. Visual signals are designed to catch the eye of the searcher. They provide contrast in the form of color, shape, or movement. The best ones employ all these. Aural signals are meant to emit sound that is louder and carries better than your own voice. They are designed for use when ground searchers are looking for you. Electronic signals are more sophisticated and more expensive than the other two but offer real advantages in range and versatility. They are worth the cost for some applications.

The ultimate goal of all signals is to make you stand out from your background. They do it by increasing contrast and range. If you were sprawled on a snowy slope with a sprained knee and saw other skiers across the canyon two miles away, it would do little good to wave a white handkerchief or to light a white smoke flare. However, you might succeed in using the shiny, plastic surface of your ski to flash sunlight into their eyes and bring them closer to investigate. Possibly a whistle blast would carry far enough and would certainly contrast with the stillness of the mountain air.

If you get lost while hunting, firing the traditional three shots into the air during the height of the shooting hours offers no contrast. Everyone is shooting then. Those same three shots fired after dark might get plenty of attention — at least from some alert game warden.

I know a man who is alive today because he used a white tee-shirt to increase his contrast with the dense green jungles of North Vietnam. Fortunately, the "good guys" saw that waving white flag before the "bad guys."

There are many effective and compact signals on the commercial market. Sporting goods stores, marinas, backpacking supply houses, and four-wheel-drive centers are good places to look for them.

Flares of various types are the most popular signals. They come in day and night styles and have the advantage of convenience. On the other hand, they are one-shot signals; once you have fired a flare, it is gone. If you fail to draw attention to your predicament, you will have to use another flare or a different signal.

The better flares are self-igniting, usually by means of some sort of pull-lanyard striker. Day flares emit dense clouds of red, orange, or yellow smoke. They contrast well with almost any background and provide the additional eye-catcher of motion as the smoke billows out and catches the wind. Unfortunately, manufacturers can pack just so much smoke chemical into a reasonably small container.

Probably the king of flares is the old standard "day-night" model, made to military specifications and accepted by the Coast Guard. It is about the size of a stubby "D-Cell" flashlight and contains two flares which ignite when their respective lanyard is pulled. The "day" end emits a large orange smoke cloud that is visible for miles under good conditions. The "night" end burns with a blinding red flame that is almost impossible to miss. These flares are waterproof (in fact they will burn underwater) and very rugged. Try marine supply and diver's shops for them. Expensive but unbeaten for reliability, they are well worth the price.

Probably the least expensive flares are the common railroad fusee and highway flare. They are less than an inch in diameter and come in several lengths. Those designed for railroad use have a sharp spike at one end and can't be recommended for general use. These flares have a striker built into their red paper casing. Most auto accessory shops sell them. Highway flares have a bright red flame with a long burning time. They are best at night but bright enough to be fairly effective in daylight. Your car should not be without them.

Even a flat tire on today's super highways is a survival situation. A couple of these flares spaced out behind your car while you change the tire can save your life by diverting high-speed traffic.

Some of the other less expensive flares have a fuse or wick that must be lighted. They are not quite as weather-proof as the sealed, self-lighting styles; but they're okay as long as you remember to carry matches in a watertight case.

Gun-launched flares have the advantage of greater range and better visibility than hand-held types. They are especially popular and effective for use aboard boats. Current legislation restricts their availability.

All flares share one limitation. They have to be used at the right moment — just before or just as the searcher looks in your direction. Firing a flare just *after* a search plane passes overhead is a disappointing waste.

The signal mirror is one of the most effective of the day-time signals. Mirror flashes have been seen from the air for over forty miles, and twenty-five miles is quite common. There are several styles and sizes of signal mirrors on the market, but they share common features. Each has a flat, reflective surface and some sort of sighting device which makes it easier to hit your target with the reflected flash.

Mirror flashes are most effective in relatively open terrain for ground-to-air signaling. However, they will also work for attracting the attention of ground searchers. Even on

bright, overcast days you can use a mirror effectively.

Commercial signaling mirrors come with printed instructions telling you how to use the aiming device. But, any mirror or shiny object can become a signal mirror if you use the following method for sighting:

Face the mirror surface toward the sun and flash the reflected spot on a nearby object. Raise the mirror to your eye and reach out as far as you can with your free hand and "capture" the spot of light in the "V" formed by your extended thumb and fingers. Now turn your whole body and the mirror together, keeping the spot of light in the "V" until the target is also in the "V." The reflected sun spot will be right on target. Wobble the mirror very slightly to cause the spot to flash off and on. The combination of brilliant light and movement is hard to miss.

Even when no rescuer is in sight, practice scanning the horizon or surrounding hillsides with mirror flashes. Searchers can see your flashes farther than you can see the searchers.

Chemical lights offer one of the newest innovations in survival signaling. These fluid-filled tubes emit a ghostly green light after they are bent to fracture an inner vial of luminescent material. They're not extremely bright, but when combined with movement, they offer a convenient, unique signaling option.

Sound signals can be highly effective when there are ground searchers looking for you, or when you are trying to get your group back together. One of the best is the standard police whistle. Its high pitch and warbling effect (caused by the cork ball inside the whistle body) carries quite well and is far more durable than the human voice. When you are nervous or scared, your voice will wear out quickly.

Even better than whistles are the compressed gas-powered horns sold for athletic events and boats. These are fairly compact and, because of their lower pitch, carry farther than whistles. The smaller ones are compact enough to be practical for many outdoor uses.

Car or boat horns can be useful signals, too. A series of three blasts, repeated at regular intervals, will help searchers home-in on your disabled rig. Firearms are okay, too, as long as you fire them at equally spaced intervals and at a time when someone is likely to notice.

Electronic devices may emit visual or aural signals. Strobe lights work much like the electronic flashes for cameras. When you switch on a survival strobe light, the battery charges a condenser which then discharges rapidly through a flash tube producing a blue-white flash. The process repeats automatically, about fifty times each minute until you shut off the switch or the battery dies. Strobes are extremely bright, but the duration of any single flash is very short. They don't offer quite the range of the better night flares, but they last a lot longer. Survival strobe lights are waterproof and rugged.

Other electronic devices include beacons, emergency locator transmitters (ELT) and two-way survival radios. These are special application devices. Beacons and ELTs transmit a beeping tone on the international radio distress frequency. They can be carried in a pocket or a pack and switched on manually in an emergency. For aircraft use, they can be rigged to transmit automatically upon impact. They would certainly be a worthy additon to a far-ranging wilderness trip.

A young lady on a solo pack-train trip in the California mountains was rescued after severly injuring her back in a fall. An ELT signaled her emergency and led searchers to the rescue. However, beacons and ELTs are expensive for wide application with the casual outdoorsman.

Still more expensive are two-way survival radios. They have been extremely successful in military combat rescues where exchange of information between survivor and rescuer may be vital, but their cost argues against use by the general public.

One exception is the popular Citizen's Band radio. Mounted in cars or boats or carried walkie-talkie style, CB's can be worth their weight in pure gold. Channel 9, the CB emergency frequency is monitored by volunteers in many areas, and a call may bring help. Even the other channels, normally used for casual chatting, can be used to get assistance.

Fred always carried a CB walkie-talkie in his day pack when he went into the mountains. Every evening he made a point of contacting some other CB'er to relay information to his family, to check the weather forecast, or just to chat. When his van got hopelessly snowbound on a high ridge, Fred was in a tough spot.

By morning the unexpected storm had dumped so much snow on the mountains that walking out was virtually impossible. However, the ridge top that had trapped Fred was a perfect spot to use a radio transmitter — there were no obstructions to reduce the radio's range. Fred's call for help was relayed by a nearby volunteer CB REACT unit, and he was whisked off the ridge by helicopter. His vehicle stayed up there until spring.

CB radios are well worth the money!

But, suppose you need help and have no signals. No need to despair. You can improvise effective signals. We've already looked at one — the improvised signal mirror.

The fire you build for reassurance or warmth can be a good signal, too. Simply make sure that it contrasts well. It should be highly visible and must be different from other campfires in the area. Remember, a search plane pilot may fly over hundreds of square miles looking for you, and there may be dozens of other fires to distract him.

One way to stand out is to build *three* signal fires, set at the corners of a large triangle, about 150 feet apart. That is an international distress signal. Keep the fires bright at night and smokey during the day. If a triangle is impractical, use a straight line. The key is to make your fires different — and a set of three fires in a geometric pattern is very unnatural. It will get attention.

Another way to get attention is to make your smoke a different color. Most burning wood produces white smoke – so make yours black. You can make black smoke by burning oil from your car, boat, plane, cycle or snowmobile engine, tires, fan belts, radiator hoses, or boot heels will work, too.

If a search plane comes close, you can hold one of your smoke flares in the campfire smoke and turn the whole column red or orange.

You can also stand out by making *lots* of smoke — so much that no one could mistake your signal for a peaceful campfire. One way is to pile green leaves, green evergreens or wet leaves onto the fire when you hear planes. Another technique is to build a Canadian smoke generator:

> Make a tripod of six-foot poles with cross pieces about halfway up. Lay green sticks on the cross pieces to form a platform. Build a fire on the platform, complete with tinder, kindling and sustaining fuel. Don't light it. Thatch the tripod above the fire with evergreen boughs hung butt upwards. The device will shed rain, and will blaze up quickly when you touch a match to it, producing a dense cloud of white smoke.

Another quick smoke producer is the "evergreen torch." Cut a small, very dense evergreen and move it to a clearing. Stand it up and build a fire around and under it, using your best fire building skills.

When searchers are in the area, light the fire. Smoke will form quickly.

You can also create contrast for yourself by using shadows and geometrical shapes. Straight lines are uncommon in nature, so anything you can build with them will be noticeable from the air. Rocks laid out in a long line in a meadow, or logs laid end to end, or sod clumps turned over and lined up, will all do the trick. If you orient your line so the sun will cast shadows on one side of your line, so much the better.

In snow, you can tramp out your lines so the sun will create the shadows that help them show up. There is nothing wrong with the classic SOS either. Big, snow letters have gotten people rescued.

Banners or flags make good signals. Some years ago when I was evaluating signals for the Air Force, one enter-

CANADIAN SMOKE GENERATOR

a. HEAD HIGH TRIPOD
(use wire if available)
b. WAIST HIGH PLATFORM OF
GREEN WOOD
c. BASIS FOR FAST STARTING
QUICK BURNING FIRE
d. LEAVING A SMALL OPENING
TO START THE FIRE,
THATCH ENTIRE STRUCTURE
WITH BOUGHS.

prising group of "survivors" tied a 10-foot-long piece of white cloth to a long pole and waved it back and forth from a lush, green meadow. Flying 1500 feet above them, I spotted that motion even before their smoke column and the 40-foot-high letters they had outlined on the ground. Tests with orange cloth were just as effective.

Moving signals work! An Alaskan pilot was rescued because he tied two red plastic jugs to long poles, then spun the poles to fling the jugs in a wild arc. And one pilot, severely injured in a combat ejection from a crippled fighter, was rescued when he waved his one good leg above the golden grass. His black boot was his signal.

Friends of mine who flew over the forests of Ontario used to kid the Air Rescue pilots at Duluth, "If we ever go down in the bush, just look immediately upwind of the biggest forest fire in Canada!" That's a pretty gross exaggeration — but when you're in trouble, don't sit there and stew about it. Make a fuss. A BIG FUSS!

6
FIRST THINGS FIRST

Life is a matter of setting priorities. Each day we make decisions on how to use our time, spend our money, please our boss — or family — or friends. We unconsciously rank-order virtually everything we do from "absolutely essential" to "ho-hum." The list is constantly changing.

On Monday morning, excelling on the job or in class or trying some great new recipe may be right up there near the top. By Friday noon that spot is probably occupied by planning or dreaming of some weekend activity.

Survival is no different from everyday life. It is still a matter of setting priorities — but the stakes are higher, and the feedback is quicker.

A young boy and his dad were exploring in the Mojave Desert on a hot Saturday morning. After a vigorous hike and checking out some old mines, they returned to their pick-up and got stuck trying to turn around in loose sand.

Until that moment they had only been interested in the mystique and nostalgia of desert ruins. Now their only thought was to get their truck out of the sand. They dug furiously around the mired wheels, tried to jack up the rear end, built ramps ahead of the tires — and worked up a soaking sweat. Finally, in utter frustration, they struck out on foot. They never made it. Searchers found their bodies the next day, less than a mile from a main highway.

The official cause of death was dehydration, but what really caused that pleasant outing to end in tragedy? They set the wrong priorities. The overwhelming desire to get home probably causes more problems for survivors than any other single thing. Pilots call it "get-home-itis."

There are no pat answers in survival. But let's Monday-morning quarterback this typical desert problem and see what it can teach us. Father and son were probably disgusted with themselves for getting stuck. That is a common survivor reaction. You can expect to feel guilty and blame yourself when you get into a survival situation. But if you let that feeling drive you to mix up your priorities, you can get into real trouble.

Because these survivors wanted to get home, they exerted themselves in the harsh desert heat and lost precious body water through excess perspiration. When their first attempts failed, they merely redoubled their efforts to get out. Trying to walk out in the midday heat without canteens was foolhardy — but walking _away_ from the thirty gallons of water in their camper was incredible!

When they got stuck, there was really no immediate problem. About the only hazard they faced was the hot desert sun. Attempting to dig the pickup out of the sand by building gently sloping ramps in front of the wheels and lining them with floor mats was good procedure too. But their problems began when freeing the truck became their number one priority. The hazard was heat, but they apparently thought being immobile was more pressing. When they should have been protecting their bodies from heat and dehydration, they put all their reserve of energy, body water, and brain power into getting unstuck.

Probably all of us would have initially tried to get the vehicle out of the sand. That's fine — *if* you work slowly, carefully, and avoid sweating to the extent possible. Also, if you have water, use it to keep your electrolytes in balance. If the cause begins to look hopeless, or you get fatigued, *quit*. Sit in the *shade* and rest.

If the two weary explorers had just given up before they were exhausted, taken a big drink of water, and sat in the shade until sunset, they could have walked to the highway with ease.

Normally, your number one priority in a survival situation is to protect your body.

There are exceptions though, and survival is not a science of absolutes. A moose hunter in Newfoundland fell into the water while crossing an icy stream that feeds Lake King George IV. His camp was about ten miles away by water and fifty miles by land. He was supposed to meet his guide at a designated spot on the lakeshore at sunset for a boat ride to camp.

His fall and some poor navigation had delayed him, and it was obvious he would miss the rendezvous. The guide would not wait because the rocky lake was too dangerous to travel in the dark. This cold, wet hunter had three choices. He could stop where he was, build a fire and a shelter, and spend a safe but somewhat soggy night. Or he could fire one of the pen-gun flares he carried, signaling the guide that he was having trouble; but then they would both spend the night out there. Finally, he could make a fast but tiring dash for the lakeshore and hope to signal the guide to come back and pick him up.

Body protection would have dictated getting a fire going and drying those wet clothes. Instead, the hunter ran about half-a-mile across the soft tundra and fired a flare as soon as he got to the beach. He had a cold but fast ride to camp.

Okay, let's second-guess this one. The decision to expend vital energy trying to get to the lakeshore before the boat was out of sight wasn't as foolhardy as it first appears. The hunter had had an easy day and he was in good shape, so the dash for the lake would not exhaust him. If his choice had failed, he still had an option open. He could have built a fire and shelter in the trees near the beach and still had a safe night. He really only gambled a little energy against the probability that he could have a warm bed and a hot meal.

There is a lesson in this one, too. When you make a survival decision (that is, set a priority), try to keep your options open. Frequently, you can avoid putting all your eggs in one basket.

The survivor of a subarctic aircraft accident decided that the minus twenty-degree temperature was his greatest hazard and that a fire was the most immediate way to solve the problem. His second priority was getting a shelter built. Yet he did not really _want_ to spend the night out there in five feet of powder snow. And there was a fair probability that another plane would be flying over soon.

He set priorities that met the hazards of the moment and left an option open. Before he started gathering firewood and shelter material, he took off his nondescript green parka and hung it in a tree, so he could work in his bright orange coveralls. This simple decision put a rescue option into basic body protection priority. The fire and shelter were unquestionably priorities one and two — but he would be highly visible while he worked at them.

He never lit the fire or started building the shelter. The very first pilot responding to his pre-crash MAYDAY call spotted him and directed a rescue helicopter to the little clearing the survivor had chosen for his triple play. His survival episode lasted exactly fifty-eight minutes.

The rescue option had been a good one. However, if that survivor had decided rescue was the number-one priority and had ignored the fire and shelter preparations to build signals, he would have had everything resting on that decision. If the lone search plane had not flown over the spot so soon, the cold night might have caused him some real problems — especially since there was very limited daylight remaining. Building a fire and shelter in five feet of snow with numb hands, cold feet, and darkness to contend with, might have been too much.

Sometimes the question of _how_ to protect your body from survival hazards clouds the decision to make it your first priority. Two young men were crossing a small Northwestern lake in a twelve-foot boat late in fall. A skim of ice sparkled in the pre-dawn glow. About two hundred yards from shore something happened and they both got pitched into the water. The initial shock of ice water immersion is almost overwhelming. As they gasped for the breath sucked

out of their lungs by the incredible shock, both of them unconsciously set a priority.

They realized that immediate protection from the cold was paramount. The stronger swimmer of the two started for shore, swimming hard. His reasoning was probably centered on the shelter of the wooded shoreline where he could build a warm fire. The combination of cold water and strenuous activity burned up his energy reserves in minutes. He tired, his muscles cramped, and he went down.

The second survivor also placed body protection first. He noted that everytime he moved, the cold became more intense as fresh ice water flowed through his clothes. So he dragged himself partway onto the overturned boat and remained still. His body warmed the water next to his skin somewhat, and his wool clothes slowed the transfer of heat to the surrounding water. As long as he did not move, he was reducing his heat loss tremendously.

He expended plenty of energy yelling though. A lakeside resident heard the fuss and came to his rescue. The second survivor was exposed to the icy water longer than his partner was, but his manner of protecting his body was far more effective.

Of course, it's possible the strong swimmer had "get-home-itis." We'll never know.

Once you have the body protection problem solved, it is time to think about getting home. Survival is *not* living off the land indefinitely. It is getting back home as quickly and as comfortably as possible. Your goal should be to make any survival situation as easy and as short as possible.

Strange as it may seem, one of the biggest hurdles

faced by survivors is the decision to _actively_ try to get home.

A mother and her ten-year-old daughter got lost while hiking amid a maze of mountain trails. As soon as they were missed, dozens of trained searchers combed the area, calling their names. For hours no trace was found of the survivors. Finally, one of the searchers heard a faint answer to one of his calls. He found the pair, huddled in some leaves, under a fallen tree — only a few yards from the trail that several searchers had used to enter the area.

As he walked up, he heard the mother trying to "shush" her daughter. They were actually _hiding_ from the searchers! Why?

Pride is the culprit. People just don't like to admit publicly that they are in trouble. Lost hunters are notoriously bad in this regard, probably because many of them consider themselves woodsmen and cannot face the embarrassment of having people know they are lost. They have been known to hide or to sneak along behind a searcher, just out of sight, then stroll into the rescue command post or onto a road as though nothing had happened.

It appears the phenomenon is common enough that we can chalk it up to human nature. You may as well accept the probability that if you are ever faced with a survival situation, there will be a strong tendency to try to go it alone. Don't succumb. Make getting home a high priority item — and use all the help you can get.

Your next priority should be to sustain or maintain your body. One of the best ways to insure that you give yourself the chance to survive an emergency is to keep fully hydrated. It takes between two and four quarts of liquids each day to keep you at peak efficiency — even if you avoid strenuous exercise!

Naturally, we get a large portion of that in or with our food, but we still have to drink a lot of water or beverages to stay at our peak. As explained in chapter 2, the early symptoms of dehydration are vague and sneaky. Unless you are in the habit of drinking a lot of water, regardless of your activity, it is highly probable that your efficiency is marred by some lack of body water.

If an emergency strikes, and your access to water is cut off, you will go downhill rapidly. The best way to prevent survival water problems is to keep your tanks full at _all_ times. If you begin an emergency fully hydrated, you can expect to survive for about five days without additional water — even at 100 degrees in the shade. Don't prejudice your fun or your survival potential by going around with half a tank of water.

Food is far less critical than water. You can expect to survive for several weeks on nothing more than the food stored in your body. You will not be comfortable and you will lose a lot of energy, but the body machine will still function.

A Special Precaution

This can be more important to you and to those who care about you than any of the survival priorities. And it is one you can practice without ever having a personal emergency. Pilots call it filing a flight plan.

Always tell someone where you are going and when you will be back. That sounds easy. Most people just go.

However, unless someone knows where you are and how long you plan to be there, any emergency can be a long and lonely one. More on this in chapter 7.

You can survive virtually any emergency if you know the basics, keep your head — and put first things first.

7
RESCUE AND YOU

Rescue is not a one-way street. When you are in trouble, it makes no more sense to simply sit down and wait to be found than to run around aimlessly in blind panic. Teamwork really pays off in a search and rescue mission — and you are part of the team! You need to know the other players.

Bill became hopelessly lost on a wildlife photography canoe trip in a vast Southern swamp. He was no neophyte in the outdoors, and had even done some reading about survival. When Bill realized it was unlikely he could find his way out of the swamp alone, he sat on a stump and considered his situation. He knew that he would be missed at sunset and that his friends would notify the authorities to initiate a search in the morning.

He saw two immediate problems. One — avoid the hordes of mosquitoes that would come out at dark. Two — try to be as visible as possible to the searchers. Both prob-

lems seemed to dictate moving to "high ground" where there would be fewer bugs and better visibility from the air. One of the survival articles he had read stressed the value of signaling from hills or ridges. It was a tough walk, but Bill left his canoe and thrashed through the tangled vegetation for several hundred yards to a small hillock where there was a break in the trees. There he made a brush shelter and dozed off.

Bill had made a big mistake because he didn't understand the search and rescue system in the swamp. He was used to the mountain wilderness of the West, where air searches are the order of the day. His decision to leave the water was influenced by that experience, and it extended his uncomfortable survival episode.

Each state and many counties tailor their search teams and techniques to the terrain, weather, and vehicle access in their areas.

If Bill had known the sheriff was set up for a quick-reaction waterways search — even in the dark — he could have slept in a comfortable motel that night. Instead he nearly went berserk from mosquito bites and weird swamp noises, while search boats passed within half a mile of him.

Search and rescue (SAR) agencies have two distinct and separate functions. First, they are geared to rescue people in emergencies. That involves a known subject in a known location — like a flood victim, sitting on her roof surrounded by rushing water. Rescue requires fast action but relatively few people. However, they must be well trained to handle injuries, transportation, mountain climbing, emergency cutting tools for entering wrecked vehicles, and many other skills. These are the heroes of books and popular television shows. Their job is difficult, dangerous, and highly visible.

The other side of the SAR coin is search — far more mundane and frustrating. But without effective search operations, the rescue people would have few pickups to make. Searches often involve hundreds of people with varying amounts of training. This side of SAR isn't as glamourous, but it is extremely important to you. Until you are found, you have no chance to be rescued.

SAR coordinators know that the first six hours of any search are the most critical. People without survival knowledge will often get themselves into such a predicament by then, that rescue is far less likely. As a result, SAR folks pull out all the stops to locate you _fast_. That means you have to start thinking about making contact with them as soon as you think you will be missed.

Your odds are a lot better if you understand the search problem. The old stereotype of hundreds of people, shoulder to shoulder, marching through the woods is an unsophisticated last ditch effort today. It is far more likely the coordinators of your seach will try to out-guess you. They will attempt to figure out what happened to you and what you are likely to do about it. With the specifics of thousands of searches stored in computer memory, they can call up similar situations, based on weather, terrain, age, experience, etc.

Analysis of that data provides a pretty good idea of where to concentrate the effort to create the best odds of finding you within six hours. It's a numbers' game. The coordinator has just so many people and so much time. He may have hundreds of square miles to cover, so he has to play the odds. Fortunately, it works — most of the time.

If Bill had done what most other canoeists did in the big swamp, he would have been found well within the six critical hours. Most people are afraid of wandering around in swamps at night and stay with their boats. The sheriff's immediate waterway search was a good bet — but Bill did not follow the pattern. They both lost the bet.

When you are in trouble and need help, take care of yourself and remember, someone is trying to figure out where you are and what you'll do. Whenever practical, stay close to your vehicle, boat, or aircraft. Searchers will almost always find your vehicle first.

You and the searchers have responsibilities to each other. You can both reasonably expect certain things of the other. According to Rick Lavalla, former President of the National Association of Search and Rescue (NASAR), you can expect them to:

Respond fast! — once they know you are missing.

Confine the search area — based on what likely happened to you and what you're apt to do.

Search at night — that's right; they'll be out there, so don't just completely hole up. You can be easier to find at night — but not if you are sacked out in a shelter made of natural materials and have no fire.

Search for clues — if you must move, try to leave notes, bits of clothing, blaze marks on trees, or arrows on the ground to mark your direction of travel.

Search with a plan and organization — don't foul them up by being rash and un-organized in *your* actions.

Use a grid search as a last resort — this is the classic shoulder-to-shoulder sweep of an entire area. When they use it, all else has failed; but it does work. Grid searches are especially effective for disabled survivors or very frightened children.

The first, hasty search will be run with horses, vehicles, airplanes or on foot right through the center of the probable search area. They will use roads, trails or streams to speed this step; and they will be looking for clues, signals or any other evidence that will narrow the search.

If the hasty search turns up some leads, the coordinators may put trackers on your trail. You can expect Indian-style trackers, trained to follow the marks you leave on the terrain, or dogs trained to follow your scent. They may even use dogs that search in a set pattern, depending upon all their senses to locate you. In either case, success is high. That means quicker rescue for you and less demand on manpower for the coordinator.

You can expect searchers to use a wide variety of vehicles. Helicopters and fixed-wing aircraft may be called into service. Four-wheel-drive rigs or snowmobiles may patrol roads and trails. Snowmobiles and horses may search cross-country, too; but your chances of quick rescue will improve dramatically if you can get on or near some place vehicles can travel. Even many of our semi-remote forests are laced with old logging roads or trails. By staying on them, you can improve your odds.

One thought to remember — if your emergency was caused by weather conditions that stalled your vehicle, searchers will probably have no better luck with similar vehicles.

The SAR coordinators run the show — so it might be helpful to know who they are. SAR programs vary from state to state and province to province. However, in the U.S. either the county sheriff or the state police will have the prime responsibility to find you on private land, national forest, or Bureau of Land Management land. If you are in a national park, the ranger usually has the task of locating and rescuing you. The U.S. Coast Guard has prime responsibility for searching along coastal waters and large inland lakes.

If you are flying when your emergency strikes, the State Aeronautics Department, Civil Air Patrol, USAF Aerospace Rescue and Recovery Service, and the county governments involved will mount a joint effort.

Many states have departments of emergency services (or some similarly named organizations) which assist local agencies in coordinating SAR efforts and in training SAR teams. Some states, such as Washington, have full-time SAR coordinators who conduct an aggressive program of public awareness, training, and integrating SAR resources in their state. If you get into trouble in these states, you can expect a top-notch, smoothly-run operation with no wasted motions.

In Canada, the Department of National Defense (DND) has the mandate for most SAR. They may not be called in on simple cases of lost sportspersons if the provincial police or the Royal Mounted Police feel they can handle the job with only ground searches. If an air search is needed or if the survivors are aircraft accident victims, the military will handle it. DND has published an excellent guide for aviators. Canadian Forces Publication 143, "Mayday, Mayday, Mayday," contains a wealth of hints for anyone, and is a must for anyone flying over Canada. It is available from

National Defense Headquarters, 101 Colonel Bay Drive, Ottawa, Ontario, KLA OK2, ATTN: DOAT 3-3.

The Western provinces have their own SAR organizations to supplement the DND. British Columbia's Provincial Emergency Plans (PEP) responds to requests for mountain rescue and various other SAR activities. Alberta has CARES (Civil Aeronautics Rescue Emergency Services) with a similar mission. Saskatchewan's Emergency Measures Air Division (EMAD) and Manitoba's Air Council (MAC) handle intraprovincial air searches. All these agencies use military search techniques and operate under control of a DND Search Master and the Rescue Coordination Center (RCC) in areas being searched.

Regardless of who is in charge, you can bet they will have a host of agencies eager and able to assist. The co-ordinator may call upon mountain rescue teams, four-wheel-drive clubs, law enforcement agencies, explorer search and rescue units, volunteer composite teams, search departments, scuba units, and C.B. radio REACT units — to name a few.

SAR coordinators can call on the military for assistance whenever they have exhausted local resources, or when the special capabilities of military units are needed. That might mean anything from a helicopter with special capabilities to a sophisticated radio net.

There has been a dramatic increase in the number of search missions conducted in the U.S. and Canada in recent years. In one Western state, for example, the annual number of searches soared from 281 to 734 in six years. Why the big jump? There are more and more people enjoying the outdoors, and they are getting farther from the beaten path. Virtually all outdoor sports are booming. To complicate the problem, we put too much faith in the equipment we use in our daily lives and in our recreation. When they fail, we are in trouble. A grain of sand can make you a survivor — if it plugs a fuel jet in your carburetor miles from nowhere. Finally, we often make bad decisions because we have to get back to work Monday morning — another facet of get-home-itis.

To help cope with the soaring SAR problem, the National Association of Search and Rescue (NASAR) was formed. It brought professional and volunteer searchers and rescuers together nationwide to share techniques and provide a voice that can be heard by our legislators and the general public. NASAR seeks to:

Mobilize public and professional support for improved response

Promote research, education, and training

Teach Americans what to do in an emergency

Get SAR forces out fast without being limited by the same factors which caused the emergency

Coordinate all available resources into statewide networks

NASAR's educational program is called Preventive Search and Rescue. The objective is to reduce the number of SAR operations launched. By teaching the kind of survival savvy outlined in this book, NASAR hopes to prevent thousands of SAR operations every year and shorten many others. All of this means that because of NASAR you can expect a quicker, more professional rescue if you get into trouble.

Many of the people involved in search and rescue operations are volunteers. Often they risk their personal vehicles and their necks to find you and bring you home. The state may pick up part of their gas bill, but most are volunteers in the purest sense. Their dedication warrants a simple action on your part.

FILE A FLIGHT PLAN

First, and foremost, always leave a "flight plan" with a responsible person. Tell them where you are going, *how many* are in your group, what they are wearing and carrying, and *when* you will be back. Include your license number, your expected parking spot, and tell them to notify the authorities if you do not call them within a specified "grace period" after your expected return. Cliff Lockett, President of Canada's Chapter of the Survival and Flight Equipment (SAFE) Association, says, "It's difficult to over-emphasize the importance of flight plans."

Suppose you leave work at 4:30 on a sunny summer afternoon and decide to detour through some beautiful woods on the way home. It is a spur-of-the-moment decision and no one else knows what you have in mind. The utter peace and beauty is just too much after a hard day at work, so you decide to take a walk. Parking the car near the road, you stride along an overgrown forest trail, savoring the sights and the smells of nature at its best.

A pretty picture, but what happens if you slip and wrench your back, and the pain is too severe to let you walk the mile or so back to the car? You will probably be missed when you fail to show up for supper, or a date, or for work the next morning. Then what? Certainly, no one is going to start searching the woods for you — at least not right away.

Probably someone will begin to worry and begin a telephone search for you among friends and relatives. When that turns up nothing, they may call the police, who will begin to look for your car. Someone will suspect foul play. County or state authorities will probably start looking for your car in more out-of-the-way places. Eventually, they will find it and start searching for you.

All of that activity takes time. Everyone is operating in the dark. There are thousands of miles of roads to cover and hundreds of square miles where you might be — and there's no hint of where to start. While the world gears up to look for you, that back is going to hurt like blazes and you are going to be mad at yourself and everyone in general for your predicament.

One quick phone call — maybe from a roadside booth — could have avoided it all. If you had told your room-mate, spouse, close friend, or someone that you were going to drive down "old 99" for a look at the fall color, your chances of spending a painful night in the woods would be almost nil. When you failed to return, at the appointed time, a more directed search could have begun. With only one route to search, the police would find the car and you in minutes rather than hours or days.

It can be incredibly hard to follow your "flight plan." It seems there is always one more ridge to cross, one more trail to check out, or another ghost town to explore. Something always tempts you to leave your pre-announced spot for one that looks better. That almost overwhelming urge to "see what's over the hill" can be tough to control. However, if you get into trouble, you'll be glad you are where you said you'd be.

One way to avoid iron-clad restrictions and still be in a position for quick help when trouble comes is to leave a

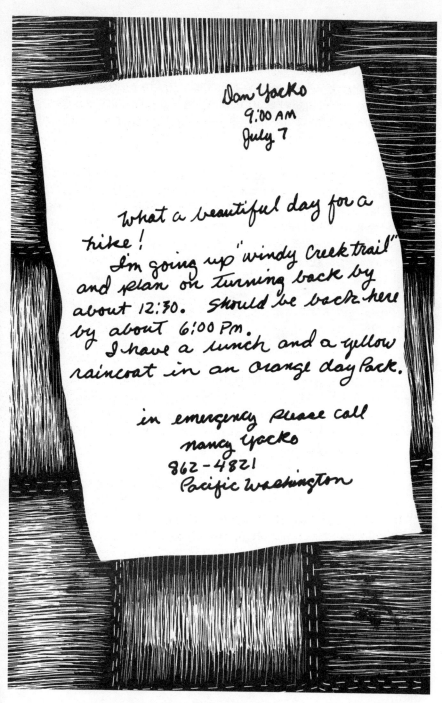

Dan Yacko
9:00 AM
July 7

What a beautiful day for a hike!
I'm going up "Windy Creek Trail" and plan on turning back by about 12:30. Should be back here by about 6:00 PM.
I have a lunch and a yellow raincoat in an orange day pack.

in emergency please call
Nancy Yacko
862-4821
Pacific Washington

"change of flight plan" in a conspicuous spot. Put a note on the dashboard of your car or some other obvious place before you leave for a new destination. Give your new plan, your time of depature and estimated return. If you are going to park a long distance from your planned spot, it is worth making a phone call from a roadside booth.

Cathy was trying out a new telephoto lens and hoping to get a spectacular wildlife shot to enter in the local photo contest. She told her roommate where she planned to park her car and the general direction she'd walk. The area was one of our Eastern national forests. As Cathy parked on a windswept ridge, she noted the valley she had selected for the photo-safari was literally filled with clouds. However, the other side of the ridge was bright and sunny. She left a match book on the seat with two words scrawled on it, "Going northeast."

About a mile into the woods she saw a huge whitetail buck and almost got his picture at thirty yards. Time after time the cagey buck let her get within good photo range and then exploded from some tangle of brush. Cathy got lots of quick shots of his upraised tail as he bounded away but nothing like what she wanted. She noted the deer was angling back toward the logging road near her car. He crossed not more than half a mile from her parking spot.

After two hours of hide and seek, there was no way Cathy was going to give up the chase just because she was now going the opposite direction from what her note said. But she was still thinking. About fifty feet from the road on a big snag she hung her yellow scarf before hurrying after the buck. Finally, the old fellow stopped to look back. This time he was in the open with a small shaft of sunlight illuminating his rack. At the click of the shutter he bolted to the right and stopped again.

Cathy made a dash to the side for another picture — and fell flat on her face. The pain in her knee almost caused her to blackout. Her foot had jammed between two roots as she fell. In minutes the sun was swallowed up and big drops of rain splattered the forest floor. She was disabled and quite far from the place she'd "flight planned" for.

But Cathy's roommate called the country sheriff when Cathy wasn't home within two hours of her estimate. He set up a hasty search of the roads and trails and soon located the car. Two searchers walked northeast, based on Cathy's note, but several others continued the road search. They spotted the yellow scarf, recalled the foot searchers, and headed into the rainy canyon. An hour later Cathy was sipping hot coffee in a warm, dry patrol car.

By filing a flight plan and keeping it up to date, first with the note, then with the scarf, Cathy had insured her own rescue. You can do the same.

TAKE PROPER EQUIPMENT

Your prime responsibility in your own rescue is to take care of your body until someone can rescue it. Make it easy. Dress for the activity and carry clothes for the environment en route. ("What to Wear," chapter 8). Carry some selected emergency equipment ("What to Carry," chapter 9).

Maybe most crucial of all — make sure you are properly equipped _inside_. Start your trip with a "full tank" of rest, water, and nourishing food. A lot of people get into trouble because they wear themselves down or use up their reserves just getting to their jumping-off point. Driving all night, drinking only coffee (or worse yet, alcohol), skipping breakfast, or launching a tough trip when you are simply out of shape is just asking for it.

LET THEM FIND YOU

Strange as it may seem, there is a tendency to *avoid* your rescuers. A former president of NASAR, says that is one of the problems facing search teams everywhere. It seems to be some sort of ego reaction. All of us feel some reluctance to admit mistakes — especially when they cause other people inconvenience, money, or personal risk.

Imagine your thoughts if you were stranded due to your error in judgment. Maybe you misjudged the weather, or trusted the old fan belt on your car a bit too much, or you failed to leave an area after being warned of an impending natural disaster. You are not hurt and you know dozens of people are out there slogging through mud and rain in the middle of the night looking for you. That is a tough nut for anyone's ego to accept. Are you going to swallow your pride and make every effort to contact the searchers? Or will you hide in embarrassment and hope to sneak out behind them?

Don't be too quick to answer that one. It is better to simply accept yourself as human, prone to make mistakes and reluctant to broadcast those which impact on others — especially when you are under stress. The tendency to cover up will be there, so why not admit it and decide right now that you will help your rescuers find you.

Think how pleased and proud they will be to conclude a well-planned and organized search. They'll be happy and you'll be comfortable — everyone wins.

STAY PUT

Survivors have a strong urge to move. Maybe we have all read too many stories and seen too many movies of people "walking out" through incredible hardships. The traditional cartoon of the gaunt, bearded survivor crawling through the desert has become an American classic. Now is the time to recognize the very human desire to move when confronted with discomfort, fear, or embarrassment. And now is the time to convince yourself to stay put.

A light plane crashed in mountainous terrain. The pilot was killed. His passenger, who suffered a head injury, wandered away from the crash site and eventually sought shelter under some thick brush. Over a hundred ground searchers and several aircraft combed the mountain sides and found the downed plane with its pilot in a matter of hours. Bad weather hampered further searching, but the SAR force stayed on the job. They found the passenger, too — 28 days later! He was dead by then, and we will never know whether his head wound clouded his judgement or whether he merely succumbed to the desire to move away from unpleasant surroundings.

There are several reasons to stay put in a survival situation. If you are with a vehicle, you are a bigger target for searchers. Also, there are limits to where any vehicle can go. When the SAR coordinator knows what kind of vehicle you have, he may be able to eliminate ninety percent of the search area and concentrate his people on where you are most apt to be — if you stay with the vehicle.

When lost on foot, there are other reasons to make yourself comfortable and stay where you are. Trying to walk out can get you hurt, especially when anxious and distressed. You are not going to be concentrating on how or where you walk. One missed step can compound your problem.

There is also a good possibility you may walk right out of the primary search area. No search can cover the whole northwoods (or wherever). If you wander into country that is not being searched intensively, there is far less chance you will be found. Finally, the SAR coordinator is using every device of technology and experience to predict where you are. Don't foul him up by wandering into some remote canyon or swamp.

Usually, it is okay to move a few hundred yards to a ridge line or hilltop where you are more visible from search planes, but even this movement has caused problems. Survivors have climbed above the altitude the search planes are flying! A friend of mine who came to grief in Alaska watched several planes fly up the valley right *below* his emergency campsite. They found Mac when the weather cleared — but that was three days later. Imagine the frustration of looking *down* on a plane that is looking down for you.

In a survival situation you may need all the energy you've got. Don't waste it traveling unless you know exactly where you are going, know how to get there, and know you can make it without exhausting yourself. Even then leave a trail; "tell" the searchers where you have gone. Write a note, blaze the trees with your knife, or mark your route with bits of clothing.

GET INVOLVED

When you are in trouble and need help, it's your rescue that counts. So take part in it! Do everything you can to be found by signaling to anything that moves. Re-read "Make a Fuss" (chapter 5) and by all means make one!

Bill did that. When morning finally arrived and the mosquitoes retreated, Bill crawled out of his shelter and spread his map, white side up, on the ground and weighted it with clods of mud. Then he gathered a huge pile of slightly soggy wood, leaves, and grass nearby. With some effort he got a smokey fire going and kept it fed with fuel. Every few minutes he created a shrill blast by blowing on the tubular cover of his camera lens brush.

Bill's SAR effort was coordinated by a county sheriff who knew what he was doing. His hasty search of the waterways failed to turn up anything. The sheriff assumed that either Bill had pulled his canoe ashore, where the brush hid it, or he had paddled into some tiny backwater that the hasty searchers had missed.

The sheriff learned of Bill's Western background from some of his friends. He reasoned that Bill might behave much like a typical, experienced mountain-area outdoorsman in trouble. Deciding Bill might have abandoned the waterways for more familiar surroundings, the sheriff launched a single search aircraft. Within thirty minutes the pilot radioed Bill's location to the coordination center. Ground SAR people had him out in an hour. Sound SAR procedures made the difference.

Bill made some mistakes, because he did not understand the SAR system in the area he had chosen for his solo-photo cruise. Those errors delayed his resuce for several uncomfortable hours. But Bill did some things right, too. He had told his friends where he was going and when he would be back. His "flight plan" got search started early and in the right area. Bill had also carried some basic survival equipment and knew how to use it. He not only let them find him, he made a fuss to insure they did so. And, certainly, he got involved with his own rescue. His signals made the difference. Without them it is unlikely he would have been spotted on that first fly-over.

You can count on the SAR folks to perform their role very professionally. Do your part to make your survival situation a short one. The only better one is the one that doesn't happen.

8
WHAT TO WEAR

It was a beautiful afternoon. Every bend in the trail brought new sights and fresh scents of mountain wild flowers. A bright June sun warmed the high meadows to nearly sixty degrees. No clouds marred the cobalt blue sky and there was not a hint of breeze. Little wonder the hikers had set off in shorts and cotton sweat shirts. Their steady climb was more than enough to keep them warm and comfortable. Even during their frequent pauses to soak up the color and majesty of high country springtime they did not get chilled.

About two o'clock a light wind began to blow from the snow fields to the Southwest. It was a bit chilly, but picking up the pace still kept Dan and Sue comfortable. Within fifteen minutes the sun was blotted out by thick, gray clouds and a few drops of rain tickled their cheeks. Dan estimated they were about five miles from the car. He knew there was a small cabin about two miles up the trail, so they elected to

continue rather than return to their Volkswagen.

Dan noted the change in aroma from the woods and meadows. "What a relief after breathing smog all week." Sue also commented on the freshness; "I always love that delicious scent in the air just before a rain, and up here it's even better." Before they could get their rain jackets out of Dan's day pack it was raining hard. They donned the colorful yellow and blue shells over their slightly soggy sweat shirts and hurried on toward the cabin.

In spite of rising wind and dropping temperature, it came as a complete surprise when Dan started shivering during their next rest break. But he laughed it off. "Guess I should have put on my rubber boots to play in the rain." Sue did not feel the cold yet, but she was concerned. "Come on Dan; let's hurry and get under cover. We don't want you sick tomorrow."

A mile from the cabin — and seven hundred feet below it — they stopped to rest again. Dan was shaking uncontrollably and his speech was slurred. "Dan quit kidding; you sound like a drunk." Sue tried to sound casual, but she was shivering too. Dan stumbled and fell twice in the first two hundred yards after the break. The second time he had trouble getting up. Sue recognized Dan was becoming dangerously hypothermic. She made a risky but correct decision. There had been a second car in the lot when she and Dan left the VW and she assumed its occupants were ahead of them and were probably in the cabin. With Sue's help, Dan crawled into the partial shelter of a large upturned rock. Sue plodded on toward the cabin. Within the hour the two climbers, who were resting in the cabin, had returned to help Dan while Sue warmed next to the stove.

This typical survival episode had a happy ending. Dan

95

took a lot of good-natured kidding, but both he and Sue learned something about clothing.

Your first defense against hypothermia and hyperthermia is the clothes you wear. Sue and Dan found that wet cotton does very little protecting — about ten percent as much as dry cotton. It would be great if we could all go about our favorite outdoor activity dressed for protection from Death Valley heat to North Dakota blizzards. Even if we could afford this kind of protection, none of us would wear the required space-man type suit. Let's face it, most of us are far more interested in how we look than in survival preparedness. However, that is no reason to forget completely that those stylish duds might have to protect your tender body.

Strive for a blend of style, comfort, and protection. It can be done! Take a look at some typical outdoor activities and see how this works.

HIKING, BACKPACKING

If Dan and Sue had altered their gear just a little, they could have avoided a potentially serious survival situation.

On any hike, other than the mid-winter, snow-country kind, it is wise to expect rain and wind. Summer storms come up fast, and they can rob you of body heat. A layer or two of wet cotton will not provide much protection and synthetics are even worse.

Wool is the magic fabric of the outdoorsman. For centuries some cultures have endured harsh environments with no protection other than wool. This natural miracle fabric has some unique properties. It generally has a lot of insulating dead-air spaces between its fibers. It retains much of its insulating value even when wet. Finally, it tends to shed water because of its lanolin content.

If Dan and Sue had replaced their cotton sweat shirts with loosely knit wool sweaters, they would have been just as comfortable during the exertion of their climb. Yet their rests would not have been chilling. When they donned their windproof rain jackets, the air trapped in the sweaters (with no wind to disturb it) would have provided excellent insulation.

The most fashion conscious hiker will have to admit that a colorful wool sweater is at least as good looking as a cotton sweat shirt. By combining a wool sweater or shirt with a wind-rain jacket and a wool stocking cap, you have taken care of almost any summer threat to your upper half. Why the cap? Because you can lose about three-fourths of all the heat your body can produce through your unprotected head. That is why survival instructors say, "When your feet get cold, put your hat on!"

Shorts are fine for hiking or light climbing, but they leave a lot of leg exposed to lose heat in a cool-wet environment. One of the easiest ways to overcome this limitation is to carry a light pair of wool trousers in your day pack. When the weather turns, just stop and pull them on over the shorts.

The cleverest solution I've seen to the shorts problem was conceived by a sharp Colorado girl. Gail made her hiking shorts out of a pair of soft wool flannel trousers. She cut off the legs and installed a round-the-leg zipper on each. A one-inch flap of material extended below the zipper on each leg of the shorts to protect her thighs from the zipper teeth. Carrying the "legs" in the day pack, within seconds the shorts can be converted into warm survival pants.

Another possibility is to carry a compact raincoat or pair of nylon rain pants in your pack. Neither is quite as good as wool pants, but both provide some protection.

DRIVING

Driving is one of the biggest challenges when it comes to "be prepared" clothing. We usually dress to arrive, not to drive. If our destination is a business meeting or a luncheon, we probably wear business clothes. We wear sport clothes to a picnic and formal attire to a concert. The point is we rarely think about the environment we travel through. We may cross a five-thousand-foot mountain pass on the way to the picnic or meeting, but it doesn't register as semi-arctic. It may not dawn on us that our shorts and T-shirt will not be much protection on the desert between Indio and Blythe.

Cars are necessary conveniences, and we cannot really dress to match all the potential hazards on a trip of even a few hours. There is an answer, though. Use the trunk.

Instead of trying to match your clothes to the multi-faceted environments your car will carry you through, simply toss some extra clothes into a box, bag, or suitcase and stow them in the trunk. Let's take a "for instance."

Suppose you live in San Bernardino and you regularly drive within a two-hundred-mile radius of there. Within two hours you can drive through desert heat of one-hundred and twenty degrees or face an occasional snow squall in the mountain passes. By putting an old hat, and out-of-style coat and a pair of sturdy shoes or boots into the trunk for each passenger, and keeping a couple pairs of sunglasses in the glove compartment, you can set out for any destination in the area in any clothes that are appropriate for your destination without being concerned about a breakdown.

This concept is especially apt in blizzard country or when driving over mountain passes. You really cannot dress for survival and be comfortable in the car, but you can load the trunk with coats, caps, mittens, and boots — even a sleeping bag or two. Being stalled in a blizzard with the right company and a trunk full of goodies could be fun.

CROSS-COUNTRY SKIING, SNOWMOBILING, SNOWSHOEING

Dressing in anticipation of snow-time survival is easier than trying to cope with the cold, wet environment of the western slope of the Cascades or with late fall and early spring in much of the U.S. and Canada. In cold, dry weather, down clothing and down substitutes are best. Nothing beats prime goose down for maximum insulation per pound of garment. However, the newer synthetics are very close and have one big advantage. If you get them wet, you can squeeze the water out and they will fluff up again to provide pretty good protection. Wet natural down is a disaster.

Snowmobilers are usually well dressed for survival simply because their sport exposes them to high wind chill most of the time, and there is little muscular activity to compensate for the cold. If you are dressed to stay really warm during an all day ride, you have little worry from the clothing standpoint if your machine quits or you get hurt miles from nowhere.

Cross-country skiers and snowshoe buffs have a far different problem. The strenuous activity of either sport demands lightweight, well-ventilated garments to prevent sweating. However, if you are hurt or isolated by an avalanche or broken ski, those clothes don't begin to offer the protection you will need for a night in the woods.

Wool is best for the active part of either sport, but since

you have to carry some extra layers for long stops or possible survival, weight becomes a big factor. Down parkas, sweaters or vests with nylon shells are hard to beat. These compress into very small bundles. Buy them with "stuff bags" if possible, so you can carry them without using too much space in your day pack. My two-inch thick down vest goes into a three-inch diameter stuff sack that is ten inches long. When I stop to rest or to fix a trail-side lunch, I slip on the down outer garment to avoid cooling off too much.

Snowshoeing usually calls for fairly rugged footwear. If you have selected good boots, the final item in your survival-clothing wardrobe is covered. Just remember to stuff a couple pairs of clean wool socks into your day pack. Then if you have a problem that requires you to spend the night, remove the socks you've worn all day and put on the dry ones. The difference in warmth is quite dramatic. Even wool loses some insulation when it's dampened by perspiration. Also socks that have been worn all day tend to get compressed and lose their loft — and the insulating air that was trapped in them when they were dry and fluffed.

Unfortunately, the footgear used by cross-country skiers is not as well suited for the unexpected night in the woods. The popular light, low-cut boots are designed for relatively steady striding. You will need more protection if you are forced to stop for several hours. Obviously, your day pack would not be very comfortable with a pair of snowmobiler's boots inside, but you can carry survival foot protection. The answer is a pair of leather and canvas mukluks. You may have to look around a bit to find them, but they weigh only a few ounces and provide excellent protection.

If you are inactive or off your skis for over an hour, it's best to remove your ski boots, put on dry socks, and don the mukluks. If the muks are going to get wet, a modern-day

Eskimo trick keeps you dry even if they get wet.

Simply pull a plastic bag over each foot after donning your socks and _before_ the mukluks. The leather and fabric will get soggy but your feet will stay quite dry. Naturally, you'll want to limit your activity so your feet don't sweat too much because the bags keep perspiration in as well as they keep water out.

One final note: You may like to wear only a headband over your ears while on the trail, but always carry a cap for stops and emergencies. Stocking caps and the European style knit ski caps are tops for warmth.

Gloves are fine when you're moving, but when you stop for long on a cold day, those individual fingers are hard pressed to stay warm. A pair of knit wool or down mittens are a wise investment. The comfort they offer far outweighs the few ounces in your pockets or pack.

FLYING

If you fly regularly, you have a special survival problem. The speed and freedom of your magic carpet take you over a wide variety of environments, and it is next to impossible to dress for them all. Also, the warmth and comfort of the cockpit tend to make us forget just how miserable we might be after an unplanned landing.

Suppose you are planning a September trip from the Midwest to Southern California. You may fly over Iowa cornfields, arid semi-desert sandhills in Nebraska, Colorado's high plains, the Rockies, some true desert, and finally horizon-to-horizon city. If you have to land unexpectedly enroute, you could be uncomfortable.

Let's just say the weatherman blew it and you find yourself in a heck of a snowstorm over the eastern slope of the Rockies. With all the "cumulo rockus" around, you wisely decide to land. Fortunately, there is a strip almost directly below you. Unfortunately there's not a soul in sight, and four inches of snow covers the little Forest Service runway. You may not enjoy hitchhiking to town in a business suit and dress shoes. Of course, it could have been worse. Not all unplanned landings are made on prepared fields.

Diversity of environmental problems complicates the "what to wear" problem for pilots and passengers in light aircraft. Fortunately, there are some ways to cope with it. One of the easiest answers is to wear a flying suit like military pilots do. The utility of multi-pocketed coveralls is hard to visualize until you have tried them.

By merely pulling on a coverall before preflight, you protect your clothes and enhance your chances for survival. A few years ago a solo pilot found himself on the ground, unhurt, in remote forested country. He had carried a survival kit in his single-engine plane, but lost it in the fire that followed the crash. The temperature where he landed was far lower than what he had experienced at his takeoff field. He wore a bright orange flying suit and jacket over some fairly warm clothes. Even though he was in deep snow and sub-zero cold, the suit's unbroken additional layer kept him warm. Searchers found him working on his campsite with his jacket hanging in a tree. He would have been okay even if rescue had been days in coming.

If you have ever dropped something on the cockpit floor while flying, you will appreciate the pockets in a typical flying suit. You can keep them stocked with all the maps, computers and goodies you need in flight and keep your cockpit neater. An ex-military pilot I know was delighted to be able to fly in sports clothes in his job as "Eye in the Sky" for a radio station. But within months, he bought a flying suit much like the one he had worn in the Air Force. Survival was no problem in city flying. He just could not stay organized and comfortable without the convenience of a special pocket for everything.

With a good quality flightsuit as an outer layer, even a business suit becomes an acceptable survival garment for moderate temperatures. If you fly over really cold areas, carry a set of quilted, insulated underwear. It weighs very little and offers super protection. When you fly over wet regions, a long plastic raincoat can be a big asset. It's handy, too, when you have to tie down your bird during a downpour.

In either hot or cold weather you will need head protection. Stocking caps are compact and easy to stow. They are great for cold temperatures. For over-desert flights a wide-brimmed hat is an excellent idea. especially the straw variety. Actually, a straw hat will do a credible job of keeping your head warm, too. They're excellent for a wide temperature range from very hot to around freezing.

With a flying suit, insulated underwear, and a good hat, you are almost prepared for a survival situation. But you will need boots. This is the only clothing item that is really a weight problem. If pounds are critical in your plane, wear boots instead of shoes when you fly. That way the additional weight is insignificant. There are sturdy boots available that are dressy enough to wear with a business suit. Western pilots often wear cowboy boots with almost anything. They aren't bad as survival protection either. If you have room to stow a pair of boots, it is better to get a pair of lug-soled, lace-up boots about eight inches high and stuff them with extra wool socks before you pack them into the aircraft.

Don't forget your passengers, either. Remember they are your responsibility. Extra clothing items may make a big difference.

BOATING, FISHING, RAFTING

Waterborne sports require special attention if you are to be prepared when an emergency strikes. Most of us tend to think drowning is the number one hazard in water survival. However, drowning is an easy danger to control. Carrying Coast Guard approved, personal flotation devices (PFDs) at all times and _wearing_ them when there are special hazards can just about eliminate the danger of drowning.

The insidious problem in most water emergencies is hypothermia and the muscular cramps that may accompany it. Water transmits heat away from your body more than two hundred times faster than air at the same temperature. That means you can die in as little as three minutes in freezing salt water. Even in "warm" water your body is losing heat amazingly fast.

Ever wonder why good swimmers drown in boating accidents? Strong swimmers are lost when others survive, because they often do swim. With the tremendous cooling rate of water on your body, exercise does not keep you warm. The movement circulates the water and makes you lose heat and energy faster.

Being a fine swimmer is not protection enough for water emergencies. You need clothing that will keep you warm and help you stay afloat.

The very best protection from the chilling effects of water is an anti-exposure suit. Such suits are essentially rubberized-cloth bags with arms and legs. The suit keeps you dry and the clothes you wear under it keep you warm.

They are bulky, hot and vapor proof. Your sweat can't evaporate; hence they have earned the nickname of "poopy suit." They're practical only for very special circumstances and very high risk.

Not quite as effective, but more comfortable to move around in is the scuba diver's wet suit. These form-fitting, neoprene-foam garments are the most effective practical protection from the hazards of cold weather immersion. The closed-cell foam traps air and insulates you from the water. What little water gets between you and the suit quickly warms up. Wet suits are expensive, but if you canoe over frigid waters or take your small boat off the coast, the investment is a good one.

If the risk factor of your water sport doesn't call for this much protection, there are other ways to ward off cold water.

Wool clothing provides insulation, even when totally soaked. You can have some of the protection of a wet suit by wearing snug fitting sweaters and pants. Turtle necks extend that protection a couple of very critical inches in an area where you can lose a lot of body heat to the water lapping at your neck. Wool socks, gloves, and a knit stocking cap top off this poor man's wet suit.

Make the stocking cap one of the long, ski mask varieties, also called balaklavas or toques. If you get pitched into the water, just roll the toque down over your face and neck. I've used these instead of a wet suit hood while scuba diving in the Pacific. They are almost as effective as three-sixteenths of an inch foam.

Fit is important for any clothing worn for water sports. By keeping it snug but not tight, you will be unrestricted in enjoying your sport and still keep to a minimum the amount of water that gets between you and your clothing if you get dunked. That is important. Your body cannot heat up gallons of water slopping around inside loose fitting clothes.

If you end up floating in cold water, don't move any more than absolutely necessary. Double up into a fetal position and remain still. Every motion pumps cold water through your clothes.

A recent innovation is the float coat with insulated waterproof hood and lining that works like a wet suit. Some float coats even have flaps which snap together to provide lower body protection. One manufacturer claims nine-and-a-half-hour survival time in fifty degree water. That's excellent.

There's also a new wet suit you can wear over your clothes. Obviously, this assumes you'll have some warning before you get dumped into the drink. The idea is to have one handy in case of emergency. If your boat catches fire, or starts sinking, you pull the suit on over your clothes, zip it up and have much of the protection and flotation of a diver's wet suit.

Neither the float jacket nor the life support suit is cheap; but for the serious water sportsman who ventures out in any but tropical waters, they represent the ultimate in style and safety.

Whatever your favorite outdoor activity, remember the clothes on your back are your first line of defense in an emergency. Give them some thought. Use these examples — and some ingenuity — and develop a wardrobe for your sport and your area. Merely wearing the right clothing can turn a potentially serious event into a "piece of cake."

9
WHAT TO CARRY

Gene and Rick were attending a convention in a large city. Taxis were hard to come by and the weather was lousy. After one late-night session, they had to wait outside the convention center for nearly an hour in a cold rain. While people around them, without raincoats, stood soaked and shivering, Gene and Rick, also without raincoats, were warm and dry — they used their survival kits. They never go anywhere without a large plastic garbage bag carefully folded up and slipped into a pocket. The bag takes up little more room than a handkerchief, but it provides an instant shelter, windbreak — or with a hole in the corner for your head — it makes a fine raincoat.

Survival kits don't need to be expensive, bulky, or heavy. They do need to be tailored to your activity, your needs, and the weather in your area. The kit should be convenient to keep with you so it's available when you need it. Even the most minimal kit can save the day.

111

Larry and Jean were hiking in the Southern California hills near Camp Pendleton. They underestimated the harsh drying effects of low humidity, temperatures in the nineties, and climbing back out of a steep canyon. By the time they slumped in the shade of their four-wheel-drive rig they were feeling sick, and Larry had a throbbing headache. They were dehydrated. Both drank heavily from the big canteen behind the front seat, but the water really didn't help much. Jean suspected that Larry had lost too much salt during his sweaty climb. She broke open their vehicle survival kit and gave him a can of slightly salty, sun-warmed beef vegetable soup. Larry told me he could almost feel that salt going into his bloodstream. They both finished the day as actively and enthusiastically as they had begun it. No survival episode this time, but the survival kit made the difference.

A homemade kit has some real advantages over even the best designed commercial models. It can be tailored to your needs, your sport, and your area. Even more important, you will know each item and why you included it. That is far better than breaking open a store-bought kit during an emergency and being surprised by what's in it — or what is not there.

Start with a container. That may sound backwards, and you may prefer to assemble your components, then search for something that will hold them. However, the activity frequently dictates the maximum size and weight of the kit, so I prefer to start with a convenient container. After all, the goal is a kit you will _always_ carry, not an exotic stay-at-home one.

For hikers, hunters and camera buffs, a small, sturdy day pack is hard to beat. They are versatile, easy to carry, and serve double duty by carrying camera gear, extra clothes, and a hearty lunch. Look for strong construction, reinforced stitching at stress points, padded straps, and brightly colored fabric. The color makes you just a little easier to find — and helps keep the kit from disappearing if you set it down and wander off to shoot a picture or pick some berries.

Day packs work very well for skiers, too, but the "fanny pack" or belt pack may be even better if you dislike having weight over your shoulders. A good belt pack will hold almost as much as a small day pack, with practically no restriction to your mobility. Members of the U.S. Ski Patrol have used these for years. Watch for sturdy construction, a rather boxy design that tapers away to nothing at the ends near your hips, a rugged, full-length zipper, and a wide belt with a secure buckle. With either belt packs or day packs, it pays to shop around as prices vary widely.

When you are searching for just the right survival gear container, don't forget your pockets. The advantages are convenience and security. There is little chance of losing your survival items. That can happen with container kits when they are left behind for "just a few minutes" to make a short side trip, check a spectacular view, or just to flex some weary muscles. All too often that is when problems occur. It's easy to get hurt or forget where you stashed the pack and be left without any supplies.

By scattering survival items throughout your clothing, you can avoid the lost kit syndrome. Remember, the best survival kit is not necessarily the one that is most complete — it's the one you have with you when you need it.

The one time I really needed a complete survival kit, I lost it in an aircraft accident. The extra stuff I had scattered throughout my pockets proved to be quite adequate. It may be wise to put some of your "eggs" in a different basket, especially if you fly or if you carry a pack that's set aside occasionally.

For aircraft survival kits, split your equipment at least two ways. Put the bulky items in the kit that stays stowed in the baggage compartment or under a seat, but carry your critical personal survival items on your person. Too often a forced landing ends up with a fire that prevents recovery of the survival kit. Then it is awfully nice to have the really important items fastened to you when you run from the wreckage.

Canvas or nylon duffle bags or lightweight aluminum boxes make good aircraft kits. Keep the weight to a minimum and make some provision for a quick-release tie-down. A loose survival kit, flailing around the cockpit in rough air or during an emergency landing, is just as bad as one you can't release in a hurry when there are flames licking around your ears.

If you wear a flying suit, you can stow a lot of the really critical items in your pockets. However, by far the most comfortable and practical way to carry them is in a fisherman's vest. These are lightweight, multi-pocketed, and will hold an amazing array of life saving items. The first few times you wear one you may find it a bother, but you will get used to it in a hurry. I've worn one for years and find the more remote the area I'm flying over, the better that vest feels. I wouldn't be without one.

Auto survival kits can be the most versatile of all. Weight is usually no object, so anything that will hold the gear you need and not rattle around will fill the bill. Old suitcases, duffle bags, cardboard boxes, or small packs work just fine. Even the best of car trunks often leak dust, so it is important to use a container that will protect your spare clothes and survival gear. In four-wheel-drive rigs the kit should be fastened to the floor or seats. A sturdy plywood box bolted to the floor and secured with a padlock is hard to beat.

Bicycles and motorcycles call for a "hybrid" approach. You can use saddlebags or other attached containers; but if your bike is a stripped-down, lightweight model, it may be best to carry the essentials in a belt pack or day pack.

Snowmobiles usually have some place you can attach or stow a fabric container of some kind to hold the gear demanded by this far-ranging sport, that's at its best far from civilization. Tailor the size and complexity of the kit to the kind of snowmobiling you like best. If you roam far and wide on remote trails, you need some pretty extensive gear. If you stay near the plowed roads, you can get by with less.

Boats and canoes require special treatment. Their survival containers should float when fully loaded and keep their contents dry. Rubberized-fabric sacks work well, although you can do almost as well with heavy-duty plastic bags. Use two of them for each container and seal them carefully. Two layers will usually keep the water out. Bright colored plastic is best, because in cold water you don't have time to search for a drifting survival kit. Surplus military ammunition cans or other tight-sealing metal containers make good boat kits, too, and have the advantage of serving as an additional seat or a cooking pot in an emergency. They should be painted day-glo orange or yellow.

The decision to fasten the kit to the boat or stow it where it can float-free requires some thought. In a large powerboat where fire or heavy seas are the primary hazards, you may want the kit secured; but it certainly must be easy to release and should be stowed with your flotation devices. A white-water canoe trip would probably call for all gear to be lashed down so it stays with the canoe in the event of an upset. It is easier to retrieve a canoe than a whole river full of bags and packs — one of which contains the survival items you need to get warm and dry. In a small fishing boat it might be better to leave the kit free. If you hit a rock and capsize or merely tip over while moving around, it will be easier to retrieve a floating kit than one trapped under the boat.

Once you have decided on a container that can go along on every outing, there is a danger of being swept up in a wave of survival gimmickery to the point that the proven life saving devices get left out in favor of flashy, well-advertised gadgets. One way to avoid the problem is to use a shopping-list approach to insure you cover all the essentials, then buy only what you've pre-selected.

By dividing your list into categories you can further direct your thinking and buying to insure you don't ignore basics in favor of nice-to-have gadgets. You'll need body protection, shelter, fire starters, signaling aids, some body maintenance items, and possibly something for your morale. Let's take them in that order and look at some compact, effective and (in most cases) inexpensive ways to cover these needs. Here are some suggestions for your kit:

SHELTER BUILDING ITEMS
(Chapter 3)
Garbage or leaf bags (the bigger, heavier,and brighter the better)
Space blanket
Poncho (nylon ponchos are far lighter and less bulky than the older, rubber ones)
Tube tent
Nylon cord
Wire saw
Sturdy knife (folding or sheath style)
Axe (only if you're skilled in using one — and have lots of room)

FIRE BUILDING AIDS
(Chapter 4)

Fire Starter
— Cigarette lighter with butane reservoir and spare flint
— Waterproof/windproof matches with case
— Pyrophoric metal (metal match)

Tinder
— Candles (thick)
— Natural tinder
— Commercial gel or tablets
— Homemade tinder

Kindling
— Pitchwood

SIGNALING AIDS
(Chapter 5)

Flares (pen gun, smoke, night, fusees, highway)
Signal mirror
Strobe light
Emergency locator beacon
Police whistle
Orange or yellow poncho or tarp (unless already included)
Emergency radio (expensive! but worthy of consideration
   for remote-area flying)
Flashlight and extra batteries
Sea marker dye (mostly for boat kits, but works well in ponds
   or on snow)

BODY PROTECTION ITEMS
(Chapter 8)

Sun hat, stocking cap   Wool socks
Sunglasses   Mukluks
Jacket, vest, sweater   Mosquito headnet
Poncho, raincoat, large
   plastic garbage bags

BODY MAINTENANCE AND PERSONAL ITEMS

Adequate supply of all prescription drugs you are taking
   at present
Water (if an arid area, at least a gallon per person should
   be carried)
Small sewing kit with heavy needles and strong thread
Safety pins
Pocket knife and sharpening stone
Tweezers
Water purification tablets
Fishing kit (4 assorted hooks, 50 feet of braided nylon line,
   a few split shot)
Snare wire (soft brass or thin, flexible braided steel)
First aid kit

MORALE ITEMS

Instant coffee, tea, bouillon cubes
Sugar cubes
Concentrated food bars
Hard candy
Firearm (only if you're expert in its use and would feel "lost"
   without it) (There are real problems here for interstate
   travel; check the laws.)
Inspirational reading material

AND
THIS BOOK!

Give some real thought to your survival kit. Then use it!
Replenish and modify it as necessary, and make it your kit.
The more personal it becomes and the more you use the
contents, the better it will serve you.

Finally, NEVER, NEVER go off without it!

10
BUT WHAT ABOUT FOOD

Food is critical to your survival — but not in the short term. In most emergency survival episodes the food you eat before you go afield is more crucial than anything you might forage.

In an emergency survival situation, food is one of your last worries. Yet more has been written over the years on foraging, snaring and fishing than on getting rescued.

Two factors tend to relegate survival food to the "nice to have" category. First, your body stores quite an impressive amount of food energy. People have lived well in excess of a month without eating. Even under rigorous conditions, survival histories of two to three weeks without food are well-documented. Secondly, long-term survival episodes are becoming more rare each year. If you'll just file a flight plan as NASAR recommends, there is little chance you will ever have to survive for more than a few days — and you can do that on internally-stored food.

In the short term, however, food is important to your spirits. It can be a strong psychological factor and improve your efficiency and endurance. That means if you can eat, you'll be able to do more to help yourself and "enjoy" your survival experience more. So, contrary to popular opinion, food is not vital to short term survival - but it is worthy of mention.

First, insure that you begin with a "full-tank" of energy. That means eating a well-balanced diet day to day.

Second, carry some food with you. Modern technology has made that very convenient to do. A whole host of compact, nourishing food products have appeared on grocer's and camping outfitter's shelves in recent years. It's no longer necessary to carry a soggy, squashed sandwich to replenish your energy supply during a long day away from home. It is far easier now to slip a few granola bars, breakfast bars, some freeze-dried trail packets, or a sack of trail mix into your pockets, pack, or vehicle. They will provide a fairly well-balanced snack that tastes good and helps keep you at peak efficiency all day long — and beyond.

There is one caution to be observed whenever you eat away from your usual haunts. Whether you're munching a granola bar along a beautiful streamside trail or rationing your last crumbs in a real survival episode, you have to have water to digest what you eat. If you eat when water is scarce, you will dehydrate yourself. Food can actually worsen your condition if you eat without drinking adequate water.

Assume you are stranded on an island in a large remote lake. Your boat drifted away during the night and it's unlikely anyone will check on you for about five days, which is when you said you'd be home. You have a tent, sleeping bag and some cooking gear; but your food supply was still in the boat. You are in no real danger, but you will get hungry and uncomfortable during your wait unless you forage a bit or do some fishing and snaring.

PLANTS

The easiest way to provide yourself something to eat is to forage for edible plant life. Virtually anywhere in the world you can find plants that contain some of the nutrients you need — but there is a problem.

A tremendous variety of plants, edible and inedible, can be found in each climatic zone around the world. Unless you devote years to their study you are not going to become an expert on edible plants, except possibly in a small area or zone. Certainly, there are a few plants that are so delicious and nutritious and so widespread that they are worthy of memorizing. There are many others that are good for you, but it takes time and practice to identify them. Some have poisonous look-alikes. Others are safe when cooked but are poisonous raw. Still others have both edible and poisonous parts. The common rhubarb stem makes such zesty pie and sauce, but has poisonous leaves.

The point of all this is simple. Unless you are a plant specialist by trade or hobby, don't depend on being able to identify all of the edible or poisonous plants — even in your own local area.

Fortunately, that does not mean you will have to shy away from eating plants in a survival situation. If you learn and follow a few simple rules, you can have the advantages of eating things that grow from the ground without danger of poisoning yourself. You don't even have to recognize the plants by name or appearance.

122

NO MUSHROOMS

Stay away from fungi as survival food. There are many edible ones in virtually any forest or moist grassland. Many of them are downright delicious, but as a group they share two big drawbacks. They offer little food value, and there is no sure way to tell the good ones from those which are poisonous — except by visual identification. Learning to select the right ones — without fail — is a big challenge.

If you like mushrooms, hunt them for fun; and garnish your more elegant meals at home with them if you must. But use a good mushroom identification book to visually verify everyone you use. That is the only way to tell good from bad. The tests applied to green plants do not work for mushrooms. Some of the toxic mushrooms are deadly, and no antidote will reverse or stop the damage they can do.

Mushrooms and related fungi are not survival fare!

NO BEANS OR PEAS

The legume family is not to be trusted. Many of them are poisonous, and even those we use regularly can become poisonous under certain conditions. When they grow in the same spot year after year (as they do in the wild), they pick up and concentrate minerals from the soil; and each generation becomes more toxic.

LOOK OUT FOR BULBS

Unless you can positively identify a bulb as edible, leave it alone. There are some which could really end your survival experience. Even the common tulip bulb is poisonous. There are two exceptions to the positive identification rule for bulbs. One is the edibility test which follows. The other involves similarities. Bulbs that look, smell, and taste like onions or garlic are edible.

AVOID "WEIRD" LOOKING PLANTS

Hairy leaves or stems, spines, thorns, or very shiny leaves, are all danger signs. Don't eat them. Some edible plants have these same characteristics; but by avoiding all of them, you help insure your safety. If a plant irritates your skin when you touch it, don't eat it. Skin irritation doesn't necessarily mean the plant is poisonous, but it may, so why take a chance.

AVOID MILKY SAPPED PLANTS

Milky sap normally indicates a poisonous plant, and a survival situation is no time to look for exceptions to the rule.

UMBRELLA SHAPED BLOSSOMS MEAN TROUBLE

There are fine, edible exceptions to this rule, too; but the risk is too great. To an untrained eye, the edible cow parsnip looks much like the deadly water hemlock - and they often grow side by side. Leave 'em alone.

NO WHITE, YELLOW, OR RED BERRIES

Again, you'll pass up some perfectly safe fruit by avoiding white and yellow berries but will avoid a much larger group of dangerous ones. If you eat an unidentified red berry, you're taking about a fifty-fifty chance that it's poisonous. With blue or black berries you're pretty safe. Only a few are toxic. If you don't recognize a dark colored berry, but feel you need to eat it, use the test described below. One happy note on berries — all the aggregated ones are edible. So, if you find some that are made of individual juice cells, like the common raspberry, go ahead and eat.

That's a lot of "No's". The rules are conservative and

overly protective, but there are plenty of plants left to choose from. Some of them can cause you grief, even though they fit none of the categories listed above. You can separate these from the harmless ones by using a simple edibility test. It is time consuming but effective. Actually, even the time involved can be a plus factor in a survival situation. Boredom can be a bigger problem than lack of food.

First, select one plant that's plentiful and easy to recognize. There is no use testing something too rare to provide a useful quantity of nutrition, or one easily confused with something else. Also, the test must be run all the way through on a single plant before beginning a new one.

Second, select the part of the plant that appears most palatable to you. Remember, some excellent food plants have toxic parts. Crush some of it and check the juice or sap. If the sap is clear, touch a drop to your tongue, and be alert for danger signals such as a bitter taste, a numbing sensation on your tongue, lips or mouth, and nausea.

Assuming this initial contact is successful, you are ready to try step three. Put a teaspoon sized chunk of the plant into your mouth and chew it without swallowing for five minutes. Be alert for the same danger signs as in step two. If there are still no ill effects, swallow the sample and wait eight hours.

If you still feel all right at the end of the wait, try a larger portion of the plant. About half a cup is fine. These quantities are not critical. Again, wait eight hours. If you don't get sick or suffer numbness, burning, or itching, consider that part of the plant edible — but don't gorge yourself on it. Go easy.

You will have to repeat the test for each part of each plant you select as a potential survival food and for each method of preparation. If you test the plant parts raw, eat them raw. If you boiled them first, eat them that way. Plant poisons react differently to various methods of cooking.

If, at any point, your test shows the plant will cause you grief, you have three choices: give up and try another plant, switch to a different part of the plant, or try preparing it some other way.

Parboiling and leaching are the most effective ways of eliminating undesirable effects of plant toxins. If your test netted you nothing more than a sore mouth or a bellyache, but you still feel the plants you tested are the best potential ones around, try to neutralize the poison.

You will need some sort of container for water or porous bag for plant parts. You may be able to leach bitter alkaloids out by crushing and rinsing repeatedly, in a series of changes of water. Dipping a cloth bag of crushed leaves, stems, flowers, roots, or fruit into a stream or pond will do the same thing.

If your taste buds still detect bitter elements, try parboiling. You will need a container. Boil your test sample for five minutes in each of several changes of water.

Neither leaching nor parboiling will neutralize all plant toxins — or there would be no need for the taste test. However, they are effective on about half of the common poisons found in plants.

If all this sounds like a lot of trouble, you may be happier as a carnivorous survivor.

ANIMALS
All mammals are edible — from the mouse that raids

your shelter to the whales in the deep sea. Obviously, unless you are surviving with the aid of some very special equipment, you will find it more practical (and safer) to zero in on little critters.

The snare is the simplest way to catch small mammals. To make one, you need a length of brass or steel wire with a small "eye" twisted into one end. Strong cord will work, too. Push the free end through the eye to form a loop that is just large enough to admit the head of your quarry. Secure the end to a tree, log or rock and suspend the loop at the level your quarry carries its head.

It does little good to place snares at random. To be effective, they should be set in a heavy traffic area. For this reason they are most useful with "trail" animals, such as rabbits, ground squirrels, and deer. You can multiply your odds by funneling the animal toward the snare by making a twig or brush barrier across the trail, on either side of the snare.

There are dozens of variations of the basic snare. Most involve some method of storing energy to quickly kill the animal or jerk it into the air. They usually employ some sort of improvised trigger to hold the energy source until the animal trips it. Then a weight falls or a tree springs up. You can get as fancy as you wish — there are books to explain exotic snares. However, there are just two vital rules in using snares: set them on trails or heavy traffic areas, and set a lot of them! Do not rely on one or two snares.

If you happen to be surviving in an area where tree squirrels are prevalent, you can improvise a highly productive adaptation of the common snare. Lean a two-or-three-inch diameter pole about eight-feet long against a tree that seems to have squirrel activity. Suspend a wire noose of squirrel-head diameter about an inch above the pole every foot or so of its length.

Squirrels seem to prefer to climb or descend the tree by following the sloping pole rather than using the vertical tree trunk! When they do, they are likely to stick their head through one of your snares and jerk themselves off the pole. As with all snares, the more you set the better your odds.

Another very simple way to catch small animals and birds is the box trap. Generations of American kids have caught all sorts of critters in these — from the neighbor's cat to hapless sparrows. Under survival conditions you may have to make your own box. It's easy to do. Just tie sticks together, log cabin fashion and add a top of parallel sticks. String, thread from your clothes, strips of bark or grass will work for tying.

To set a box trap, place the box open side down and prop up one edge with a stick that is just long enough to admit your prey. Place some appropriate bait under the box and tie a string to the stick. Then step back out of sight with string in hand and wait — and wait. When your supper steps under the box to test the bait, yank the string, pulling out the prop and dropping the box. You can also use a heavy flat rock or log in place of the box — then you have a manually triggered "deadfall."

BIRDS

Meat-eating birds can be caught with a fishhook imbedded in a scrap of meat and tied with several feet of string to an anchor point. Most other birds are quite easy to catch in a box trap. If they are trail runners like pheasants, snares work well. A few years ago, I watched several six-to-eight-year old kids in Korea catch big, beautiful pheasants with brass-wire snares set in brushy runs on the Island of Cheju

Do. They will never go hungry where running birds are plentiful.

FISH

If your kit includes hooks and line, you can find bait and catch fish in almost any fresh or salt water. You may have to spend a lot of time and experiment with many kinds of bait, but eventually you will entice something to bite. Remember, you are not trophy fishing. A four-inch bottom fish will taste just as good in a survival shelter as a fifteen-inch brook trout. Persistence pays. If one spot or one bait is unproductive, try another.

In small streams it is often possible to chase fish into shallow spots and catch them by hand or whack them with a tree branch.

REPTILES

Snakes, lizards, turtles, and frogs are all edible and most are quite tasty. You can catch most species by whacking them on the head with a stick. Since some snakes and a few lizards have poisonous bites, it's wise to take some precautions.

First, never hunt for snakes where the snake has the advantage. Don't climb over rocks or crevices or put your hands or feet down where you can't clear the area first. You've got to know that you can see the snake before he can strike you. Second, cut the head off any snake or lizard as soon as you are sure it is dead. Be careful, the fangs of a dead reptile are just as potent as those of a live one. One scratch can ruin your day.

Skin snakes, lizards, and frog legs, then cook them any way that suits you. Turtles are easiest to cook by simply laying them on their backs in the coals. The shell becomes the pot.

If you haven't tried fried rattlesnake, you are missing a real delicacy. A friend of mine served one on a pilaf of rice at a formal buffet. It was the hit of the meal — even after the guests learned what they were eating.

INSECTS

That's right, bugs! Insects are probably your easiest source of survival nutrition if three conditions are met: (1) you have adequate drinking water, (2) the weather and your location make them available, and (3) you can quell any aversion you might feel toward eating them. You may have little control of the first two, but aversion can be conquered.

Insects are protein-rich and a popular food source in many parts of the world. Nearly all of them are "clean" and most are quite tasty. You'll probably like them best roasted or fried, but if you're not able to cook them, you can eat them raw. It pays to be cautious with raw ones, though.

Jim was attending a survival course when he noticed his instructor sitting cross-legged near a mound, eating something. "Mmm, termites. Here, have some, Jim," he offered. Jim was squeamish, but wasn't about to show it. He picked up a single termite and bravely popped it into his mouth — and promptly let out a yell. "The little devil bit me," he howled.

That ended Jim's aversion to insects. He sought revenge by first biting the head off every termite he could catch. If you must eat insects raw, Jim's method is a good one. "He who bites first . . ."

Ants, bees, termites, grasshoppers, hairless caterpillars and grubs are all edible and highly nutritious. To roast, lay them near fire coals and cook until crispy. You can find them almost anywhere by turning over rocks, prying open rotting wood, opening anthills. Hunt insects early in the morning, while they're still cold and sluggish.

Aquatic insects are a good food source, too. You may be able to catch them in quantity in any stream by improvising a "net" out of a shirt or handkerchief. Anchor one side to the stream bed with rocks and suspend the other side several inches above the bottom. As the cloth billows out, stir up the stream bed a few feet upstream to dislodge the insect larva. The current will pin them to your net.

A few insects are somewhat poisonous; so if you venture beyond the common ones listed above, use the taste test described in the plant section of this chapter.

In all but the most harsh winter conditions there's food available almost anywhere. To take advantage of it:

— Be observant.

— Consider anything that grows, walks, crawls, flies or swims as a *potential* food source.

— Be prepared to eat anything you find!

These basics about food will help you hold body and mind together while you attend to the business of getting rescued. If you are intrigued with living off the land by "root cooking and bug eating," there are many manuals and guides available. This book deals with getting you home.

11
DEALING WITH INJURIES AND ILLNESS

Several years ago a brake failure in an old jeep thrust me into a survival episode about seventeen miles from a Colorado public highway. A sturdy pine tree stopped the runaway jeep before it plunged over a cliff into the South Platte River, but the impact left me with blood spurting from my head. It was obvious I'd severed an artery. Fortunately, Minor Nelson, my partner, knew what to do.

He pressed hard against my temples with the heels of his hands. The spurts diminished to drips, and in about ten minutes the bleeding had virtually stopped. Minor walked out for help. His knowledge had turned a very serious survival situation into an educational adventure.

Probably nothing complicates a survival experience as much as an injury. Yet many people become survivors simply because they get hurt. Even a minor injury in the outdoors can turn a pleasant afternoon into a dire emergency.

Consider the sharp pain of a badly twisted ankle that strands you miles from your camp or car. The effects may be almost entirely psychological, weakening your will to help yourself and work toward rescue, even when little real physical disability exists.

You can minimize the limitations of most injuries and some illnesses by taking simple but appropriate action. It's not likely you will be able to cure serious problems, but you can control the impact of common injuries on your survival. The actions you take in your own behalf or to help an injured partner in a survival situation are not really first aid. Courses in first aid and Emergency Medical Technician (EMT) classes deal with what to do until a doctor can take over. First aid is geared to relatively short-term treatment to stabilize an injury pending professional repair work or medication. There are two differences between first aid and "survival medicine." First, under survival conditions you don't know how long it will be until you can get professional treatment. Secondly, you may have to use or even misuse the injured part for higher priority problems — like shelter building or signaling. Your can't make treating your injury your sole function. Yet, you have to minimize its impact.

Let's look at some common survival injuries and see what you can do.

PAIN

The pain associated with many injuries is serious enough under survival conditions to warrant attention as a separate problem. Individual sensitivity and reaction to pain varies tremendously. Identical injuries in two people may produce nearly disabling agony in one, while the other suffers only minor discomfort.

The U.S. Air Force survival manual says that you can tolerate any amount of pain if your goals are high enough. That may be overstating it a bit, but keeping busy and concentrating on the business of getting rescued can certainly reduce the impact of pain. Your body announces damage or disease by flashing a pain warning. It reminds you to rest that part. Under normal conditions, this is good.

When your life depends upon your ability to deal with survival problems, you may have to ignore the warning. Survival case histories are full of instances where people did just that. Lauren Elder, survivor of a mountain plane crash, traveled twenty miles and climbed down more than eight thousand feet, including a one-hundred-foot vertical rock face — all with a broken arm. She had to use that arm even though she could feel the broken ends of bone rubbing together inside it. She kept going and she lived!

Her experience and dozens of similar ones point out some ways you can conquer pain. First, understand that pain is a signal and not dangerous in itself. Secondly, concentrate on what needs to be done. Stay busy and keep your goal in mind. You want to get home! So work at that. Don't cater to your pain when your survival is at stake. Finally, try to look upon your pain as a temporary discomfort that can be tolerated. Naturally, you want to avoid aggravating the pain or the injury that is causing it, but remember to "keep first things first."

SHOCK

Severe pain can cause shock, as can fear or the sight of a bad injury to yourself or someone else. Any of these causes may be present in a survival episode. Shock may also result from heavy bleeding, burns, allergies, or infection. The result is the same regardless of the cause. Blood circulation to the brain is disrupted, and rather predictable symptoms appear.

If you have ever experienced shock, it is unlikely you will forget the symptoms. That light-headed, weak, half sick, unreal feeling is indelible. If you have never felt shock or if you are watching for it in someone else, there are signs you can expect to see.

Any of the following may appear:

1. The skin will feel cold and clammy.

2. Breathing rate will increase, and may be quick and shallow, or irregular and gasping.

3. Pulse will be weak and rapid.

4. Nausea or vomiting is likely.

5. There will be some mental confusion.
There are later, more severe symptoms — but you have to catch and treat shock *before* they occur.

Regardless of the cause, you can use one standard treatment:

1. Control bleeding (if there is any).

2. Drink plenty of fluids. (But don't try to give them to a shock victim who is unconscious.)

3. Lie down, preferably with the head slightly lower than the feet, and rest until the symptoms pass. (If a head wound is causing the shock, don't rest head-down.)

4. Stay warm, put on extra clothes, get into a sleeping bag.

BLEEDING

Blood loss from a wound can usually be controlled by direct pressure. Certainly, that is the first method you should try. Merely take a clean pad (sterile if you have it) and press it firmly against the wound. Hold it there until the bleeding is controlled. You may have to tie or wrap the pad in place to hold the pressure.

If direct pressure doesn't work, or you can't reach the wound, you can apply pressure between the wound and the heart. Major arteries run very close to the surface at several points on your body. These "pressure points" offer an opportunity to restrict the flow of blood from the heart to the wound. You can use your hand to press against these arteries or you can push the pressure point against some padded object. Following the jeep accident described at the beginning of this chapter, Minor's timely use of the pressure points on my temples probably saved my life. I might have been able to stop the bleeding myself, using the same technique, but the fatigue of holding the pressure would have been a factor to contend with.

If the wound is on an arm or leg and neither pressure on the wound nor pressure on the artery supplying blood controls the bleeding, a tourniquet is a last resort — a desperation move. It can save your life, but it may cost you the limb if rescue is delayed very long. Tourniquets are so effective in controlling the flow of blood that they starve the limb of virtually all circulation. The bleeding will stop, but so will the flow of life-giving oxygen.

You can improvise a tourniquet from any band, strap,

PRESSURE POINTS

BONE

SKIN

ARTERY

PRESSURE POINT

belt or rolled fabric. Make a continuous loop, slip it over the limb to a point just upstream of the wound (between the wound and the heart). Pad the tourniquet then twist the loop with the aid of a stick. Tighten it down and cut off enough of the circulation to control the bleeding.

Once you have the blood loss stopped, leave the tourniquet in place. That is not easy and seems contrary to nature to leave a limb without circulation. It is a matter of choosing the lesser of two evils. If you leave the tourniquet in place, you stand a chance of losing the limb due to prolonged lack of oxygen. However, if you release it, the rush of blood into the limb can reduce your blood pressure enough to send you into deep shock — the kind you cannot take care of yourself. It is better to risk an arm or leg than your life.

FROSTBITE

When you do everything else right, there is little danger of frostbite, even under very harsh conditions. However, a small error or lack of attention can make any outdoor person a victim.

To prevent frostbite, follow the basics outlined in "Your Body is Where you Live," chapter 2, and "What to Wear," chapter 8. Check your hands, face, and feet often. At the first indication of numbness or waxy-looking skin, warm the area fast. Don't wait. Unless you catch the freezing at this early "frost nip" stage you are going to have some injury.

If you miss the early symptoms and actually freeze some tissue, you are going to have a tough decision to make. Ideally, you should thaw the frozen part as quickly as possible.

Rapid thawing is the best way to avoid permanent

damage. But it may not be the best answer to your problem. After you thaw the affected area, it is going to hurt! You can walk on frozen feet; however, once thawed, the pain will likely immobilize you.

It is a tough decision. If you need the use of the frozen limb, you may have to leave it frozen. That may increase the damage.

The best thawing method is submerging in water heated to just over one-hundred degrees Fahrenheit. Water at that temperature feels slightly warm to the inside of your elbow. When you have no water or container available, use your body heat (or someone else's). Warm frozen feet against the opposite leg or with your hands. Frosted cheeks or nose can be thawed by burying them into your hands or the hood of your jacket. Place frozen hands in your armpits or crotch.

Treat the frostbitten area as an injury — don't rub it; don't put snow on it or otherwise abuse the damaged tissue.

BLISTERS

Frostbite, friction, thermal burns, sunburns, or stinging plants can cause blisters. All are potential hazards for survivors. A blister is essentially a protective reaction over an injury. It should be left intact. Do not open or drain the fluid from blisters. Protect them with a clean dressing or padding.

Better yet — avoid blisters by protecting yourself from the things that cause them. Be extra careful and cautious in a survival situation. When you feel a sock or boot rubbing, stop and fix the problem or stay off your feet for awhile. Keep your feet dry; if necessary, take time to dry and air them periodically. Avoid hand blisters while using your knife or building a shelter. If a spot gets tender and sore, either pad it, switch hands, use a different grip, or rest awhile. To prevent blisters caused by exposure to sun, plants, heat or cold you have to protect your skin from the causes.

It takes discipline to stop and take preventive action when you are trying to get yourself rescued, but blisters are no laughing matter. Prevent them.

FRACTURES, SPRAINS, STRAINS, AND DISLOCATIONS

Although these injuries have little in common medically — other than involving the skeleton and its connective structures — they have similar effects on you as a survivor. All can cause severe pain, swelling and lack of desire or ability to use the affected part. Regardless of the ultimate diagnosis, these injuries can deprive you of part of your survival equipment. Even a sprained finger can be quite a loss when you are trying to light a fire under life and death circumstances.

Fortunately, the survival treatment for all four structural injuries is the same. There is no need to attempt an exact diagnosis. Leave that to the doctor when you get home. Don't try to "set" a fracture or "reduce" a dislocation. That is a job for a professional. Just immobilize the injury and you will reduce the pain and prevent aggravating the problem.

Hand, arm and shoulder injuries can often be immobilized sufficiently with a simple sling. You can make one from your belt, lengths of rope, a piece of clothing — anything that will form a loop around your neck to support the damaged arm. With a little patience you can make a sling with one hand. One survivor even improvised slings for _two_ broken arms. He used his teeth to tie the knots.

Splints are effective for protecting structural injuries, especially leg and foot problems. You can fashion splints from small poles, cardboard, bits of wreckage, ski poles, snowshoes — almost any rigid or semi-rigid object you can find. Always pad the splint to prevent painful pressure or abrasions. Tie the splint in place with plenty of snug knots. Treat any wound in the area prior to applying the splint.

The purpose of splinting is to immobilize the joints both above and below the injury. If that is not possible, try to prevent any movement in the injured area. If a foot or ankle is involved, keep your shoe or boot on.

When you have to get around with an injured leg or foot, a cane or crutch is a big help. A padded, forked pole will serve as an emergency crutch.

SNOW BLINDNESS

Prolonged exposure to bright light can cause damage to your eyes and needless pain and discomfort. Snow conditions with full sunlight are most dangerous — hence the name — but any bright-light situation can cause problems. When you feel yourself squinting severely, use sunglasses or ski goggles. If you don't have them, either get out of the glare or make a pair of goggles. Any strip of heavy cloth or thin bark will work. Make a blindfold, then cut narrow slits horizontally so they will be centered over each eye when you tie the strip over your eyes, "Lone Ranger" fashion.

Snow blindness is sneaky. If you fail to protect yourself, you may get through the day without apparent trouble — only to be struck by burning, watery eyes, poor vision, and headache after sundown. When those symptoms appear, it is too late to avoid some prolonged discomfort. Protect your eyes from further exposure to light by bandaging them or staying in your shelter. Cold compresses will help ease the pain.

Snow blindness will spoil the finest day in the outdoors. In a survival situation, it is disabling. When you first notice excessive squinting, act!

BURNS

Probably no survival injury is as serious and difficult to deal with as a severe burn. With anything more than a simple first degree burn (where the skin is only reddened, like a sunburn) you have three big problems. Shock, dehydration, and infection are likely to occur in that order. The shock is caused by pain and trauma to the circulatory system near the burn. Loss of body fluids in the burn area will require much higher than normal intake of water. After a day or so, the loss of skin and the favorable conditions for bacteria growth pose a threat of infection which you can't control in a survival situation.

You are quite limited as to what can be done for a burn without sterile conditions and some medical gear. As a result, it makes little difference what the medical diagnosis of the severity of your burn might be. There is not much point in trying to determine whether you have a first, second or third degree burn — you will have to treat them all pretty much the same.

Your first move, if the skin is intact, should be to cool the burn area. Don't waste time! Plunge the burned part into cold water, snow or anything you have that will chill the injury without further damage. Cooling prevents harm from residual heat in the tissues. Unless you get the temperature back down to normal quickly, tissue damage may continue for several seconds after the heat source is removed.

Clean the burn area with soap and water, but be gentle. You don't want to compound the injury by disrupting damaged tissue. Cover the burn with the most sterile dressing you can contrive. Boiled clothing or commercial dressings from a first aid kit are ideal. Do everything you can to keep the burn area clean and protected or even delay the onset of infection, you will enhance your chances for rescue and a quick recovery.

Do not use creams or other surface medications, and keep the dressing loose so you don't restrict the circulation as the injured area swells. Pain will be a problem you will have to deal with. Aspirin may help if you have it.

Be alert for signs of shock. Even if no shock symptoms occur, start drinking more water than you think you could possibly need. It will help fight shock and will ward off the dehydration that normally follows a burn.

DIARRHEA

Common diarrhea is quite prevalent under survival conditions. It may be caused by nervous tension, by eating unfamiliar foods, or by intestinal infection from contaminated water. In any case it is uncomfortable at best, and debilitating when it is severe. It causes dehydration which can only be combated by drinking what will seem like an excess of fluids.

Most diarrhea is relatively easy to control — even without access to a pharmacy. Just eat fresh (but cool) natural charcoal from your campfire. The taste is not unpleasant since all the pitch and cellulose are burned away. A couple of tablespoonsful will get you back in control.

Twice, I have had outdoor experiences marred by sudden diarrhea, once in the Philippine jungle and once in the Sierra Nevada. In each case two small lumps of charcoal eaten before bedtime had me feeling great by morning — and my sleep was uninterrupted. This old remedy works.

FEVER

Like pain, fever is a symptom of some other problem; but it can be a survival problem in itself. If you have aspirin, take it according to directions for some relief. A tea brewed from the inner bark of the willow tree will work just as well as commercial aspirin — if you are lucky enough to be stranded where these trees grow. Soaking your body in cool water can also reduce a fever.

Many survival injuries and illnesses can be prevented by keeping yourself and your camp clean and neat. That sounds trite — but it is true. The chance of getting hurt is greatly lessened when you keep everything in its place and use all your survival tools properly. By merely washing yourself and your clothes frequently — even when that seems like a very low priority item — you can reduce the odds of aggravating your survival situation.

If you get hurt or ill in spite of your best efforts, remember — your ultimate goal is to get home. That has to govern all your efforts and decisions. With that in mind, it is up to you. You're the doctor.

12
WHAT IF

There is one simple, effective way to sharpen your emergency survival skills and increase your outdoor enjoyment. It is free, it is fun, and it doesn't cost you one minute of your recreation time. The technique is so effective that it has become a basis for major portions of the emergency training of military and airline flight crews. These professionals sharpen their thinking, their procedures, their problem-solving, and their motor skills in flight simulators. Instructors present emergencies and the crews solve them in real time. The whole program develops a "what if" thought process.

Flight instructors instill similar patterns in their students when they pull the throttle to idle unexpectedly and call "forced landing." The student pilot has to find a place to put the airplane down. About the third time that happens, you start thinking, "What if that louse pulls the power off now — where will I land this thing?" Strangely, this doesn't degrade your thinking about the minute-by-minute business of flying, but it does make you aware of potential landing spots along your routes of flight.

You can do the same thing to yourself, whether you are flying a light plane, carrying a heavy pack, or gliding through deep powdered snow. Regardless of your sport, practicing "what if" can improve your ability to deal with real emergencies. In addition, you can virtually eliminate the initial rush of panic that often accompanies unexpected trouble in unfamiliar surroundings.

Suppose you are driving your car through a remote spot and ask yourself, "What if the radiator hose breaks and I lose all the engine coolant?" or "What if I blow a tire and smack into that embankment, damaging the front suspension?" Several things may happen. You might answer yourself, "Ridiculous! Nothing's gonna happen. I've driven for years without being stalled along the road." However, if you are persistant and play the "game," you will start noticing things you may have been ignoring. You may remember the first aid kit that has been in the glove compartment since you bought the car. The tape it contains could be used to wrap the split hose. Water from the ditch ("Hmm, never noticed that before") could be used to refill the radiator. You might even think, "Hey, I bet if I left the pressue cap loose, that tape would have a better chance to stay intact until I get to town."

Thinking about the bent suspension and steering system might get you off on a "How do I attract someone's attention or which way do I walk to find help quickest?" kind of daydream. You may be surprised how resourceful you are when you give yourself a problem and force yourself to solve it — without any undue adrenaline or fear.

You will find yourself applying the survival principles

outlined in this book, and in "using" them you reinforce them in your memory. The more you play the game, the more proficient and adaptive you become. Even more important, however, is that you form a habit of acting rationally and constructively in an "emergency." Nothing prevents panic like taking control of a situation. The more you practice taking charge of hypothetical (but realistic) emergencies the better you will perform in real cases.

Playing "what if" also tends to improve your confidence and to evolve a "will to survive" or "positive mental attitude." Those terms simply refer to the psychological aspect of any survival situation. Volumes have been written on the importance of will and attitude, but the bottom line is this. Your attitude will be better if you have prepared yourself physically, mentally, and emotionally to deal with personal crises. You can do this by practicing when there is no emergency.

Naturally, it would be great if you could do some actual hands-on practicing when you simulate an emergency. However, just thinking through your actions will help a lot.

Marian, Chuck, and Susan got their four-wheel-drive rig stuck in a submerged clay vein in a remote mountain creek. They were about thirteen miles from a town, almost that far from a ranch. It was raining and a cold wind was blowing down the canyon. It was a perfect setup for overwork, exhaustion, and hypothermia. But Chuck had driven those logging roads and forded the creek before — and he had "what if'd" most of the obvious hazards.

Seeing his pet rig bumper-deep in goo was a frustrating experience, and one he had been through before in his daydreams. He told the girls to stay inside where they would be dry. Then he cut a twenty-foot pole about four inches thick and used it to lever the front end up and backwards while

Marian drove. It didn't work. Real life does not always follow your "what if-ing." As soon as he saw the lever would not solve the problem, he jury-rigged the winch to pull the mired Toyota backwards. That broke the winch cable — scratch another solution that had done well in daydreams. Tying the broken ends of the cable together for another try almost got them out until the shear pin broke.

The next step in Chuck's "what if'd" scenario was to walk out, after first loading up gear from the vehicle's survival kit. There were also raincoats, ponchos, and dry clothes. The idea was to walk until one of the trio tired (probably ten-year old Susan), then stop, make camp for the night, and continue to the highway in the morning. While Chuck readied the gear, Marian tried a step from her "what if-ing." She got on channel 9 of the CB radio and called for assistance. When there was no answer, she called again "in the blind" hoping someone would hear and respond. She gave their location, the problem, requested a vehicle with a winch, and repeated the whole transmission every few minutes.

Chuck had ignored the radio. It was in his "what if" scheme all right, but he felt the mountains on all sides would swallow the signal. About 10 minutes after Marian's first call, "Clay Bank" answered, saying they knew the spot and were on the way. Clay Bank turned out to be a local rancher with a big pick-up. The Toyota was on dry ground in short order.

The point of this simple yarn is that each step followed smoothly and logically as each preceding "solution" failed. The steps had all been rehearsed before, even though the situation was new. If Clay Bank had not shown up, the trek to the highway was still a good option.

Without "what if" practice, Chuck and his passengers

might have worked feverishly trying to free their four-wheeler and used all their reserve energy while they got soaked and chilled. The combination would have almost certainly resulted in hypothermia and a critical survival situation. However, their sessions of "what if's" had programmed them to act rationally and with a plan. You could say they had avoided real trouble by pretending they were in trouble — before the fact.

John was a pretty good hunter. He thoroughly enjoyed the outdoors in general and animals in particular. He was equally happy hunting with a camera or a gun. John's job kept him hustling for long hours and still he brought work home. He was so busy that trips afield were squeezed into his schedule with little time for planning. Even in the woods, most of John's spare moments were spent thinking about problems on the job. He never even considered the possibility of trouble while hunting, certainly not on that snowy November morning.

When he stepped on an ancient three-foot-high cedar stump for a better view, John was about to become a survivor. Just as he raised his binoculars there was a muffled crunch of rotten wood. The sudden fall which followed resulted in a stab of pain in his right leg that just about snuffed out his consciousness. The horror of his situation struck him beyond reason. He yelled for help until he was hoarse, fired all his ammunition in three shot series — and crawled under a big fir tree to die. The awesome shock of being disabled and in pain in the one place he had always considered a haven from the press of daily living was too much. He felt betrayed and helpless. He didn't act — he quit.

Compare this with Gail's experience. She was an avid backpacker and got away whenever she could from her job as buyer for a big department store. Gail liked to go solo, but

she recognized the extra danger. She used her commuting time to plan her trips and to "what if" them thoroughly. During breaks along the trail she kept her mind active and off her work by asking herself how she would handle various emergencies.

When Gail broke her ankle, she was disgusted with herself for being so clumsy. She was in just as much pain as John, but she reacted as if she were using a script. She immobilized the ankle as best she could, crawled to a slightly overhanging rock face, built a fire and brewed some tea. Somehow the pain wasn't as bad while she was busy. By dark she had a shelter of sorts and enough wood to keep the fire going through the night — thanks to the crutch she fashioned from a forked tree limb. Except for the pain, she found satisfaction doing something she'd thought through for many months. There was no wasted motion — or emotion — no indecision, and no panic. Having a plan of action prevented that.

Other hikers found Gail just before noon the next day. She rode off the hillside in a helicopter. John was rescued, too; but the trauma of his ordeal had left its mark. He never again felt the same secure peace he had previously known in the woods.

"What if" pays off in emergencies.